SHARED SPIRITS

Wildlife and Native Americans

by Dennis L. Olson

NorthWord Press
Minnetonka, Minnesota

NorthWord Press
5900 Green Oak Drive
Minnetonka, MN 55343
1-800-328-3895

Designed by Russell S. Kuepper
Illustrations by Kay Povelite
Photography credits © 1995: Wiley/Wales/ProFiles West, Cover, 138-139; John Hyde, Title Page, 80-81; Bill Lea, 9, 11; Henry H. Holdsworth, 10, 132; Jeff Foott/DRK photo, 14-15; Jeff Vanuga, 16, 21, 68; Helen Longest-Slaughter/Nature Images, 17, 28-29; Michael H. Francis/The Wildlife Collection, 18-19; Alan and Sandy Carey, 22, 41, 69, 141; Raymond K. Gehman, 23; Jim Brandenburg/Minden Pictures, 24, 61, 63, 86, 87, 90-91; Joe McDonald/Natural Selection, 26; Stephen J. Krasemann/DRK photo, 27, 70; Carl R. Sams II/Dembinsky Photo Associates, 31, 65, 118; Sharon Cummings/Dembinsky Photo Associates, 32; Robert McCaw, 33, 34, 53; Rod Planck, 36-37; Bruce Montagne/Dembinsky Photo Asssociates, 39; Kennan Ward, 40, 112; Michio Hoshino/Minden Pictures, 43, 76; Tom and Pat Leeson, 44-45, 62, 72-73, 83, 93, 134-135, Epilogue; Susan Winton, 47, 48-49; Ted Nelson/Dembinsky Photo Associates, 51; Robert Houser/ProFiles West, 52; Lawrence Michael, 57; Skip Moody/Dembinsky Photo Associates, 58-59; Richard Hamilton Smith, 66-67, 85, Back Cover; Lynn M. Stone, 71, 100, 101; Art Wolfe, 75; Chris Huss/The Wildlife Collection, 77; Elizabeth DeLaney/ProFiles West, 82; Jeff Foott, 95; Tom Murphy, 92, 94; Layne Kennedy, 96-97; John Hyde/Pacific Stock, 105, 106-107; Frans Lanting/Minden Pictures 99; Frank Oberle, 108; Michael Mauro/F-Stock, 111; Michael H. Francis, 113; Stephen J. Krasemann, 116-117; Carl R. Sams II, 121, 122, 123, 127, 128-129; Craig Brandt, 133; Richard Day/Daybreak Imagery, 136; John Netherton, 131.

Library of Congress Cataloging-in-Publication Data
Olson, Dennis L.
        Shared spirits : wildlife and Native Americans / by
Dennis L. Olson.
            p.   cm.
        ISBN 1-55971-676-2 (sc)
        1. Indians of North America–Folklore.   2. Animals–Folklore.
    3. Human-animal relationships–North America.   I. Title.
    E98.F6G29   1995
    398.24 ' 52 ' 08997–dc20   95-15129

Printed in China
10 9 8 7 6 5 4 3 2

CONTENTS

DEDICATION

For Penny, first editor, best friend and shared spirit

ACKNOWLEDGMENTS

I owe a debt of gratitude beyond words to traditional Native American people. My ways of thinking, acting and being have been expanded and focused by the wisdom of my Elders. I also owe the same debt to the Animal people—the mice, deer, bears, wolves and others who have taught me to step outside of myself and see teachers in every form imaginable. Among the many human animals who have been teachers and friends are those who carry stories with them every day of their lives. Albert Hunter, Susan Strauss, Dee Bainbridge, Keewaydinoquay, Wilson Hunter, Deb Sanders, and Douglas Wood are professional tellers who have inspired me in many ways. I'm grateful to Hyemeyohsts Storm and Ruth Beebe Hill for shifting my world view dramatically back in the 1970s. Tom and Pat Klein have continued to believe in me personally and professionally throughout my adult life, and have given me the opportunity to do this book. They represent everything I know about good friendship. Jack Pichotta is a mentor as well as my friend. Barbara Harold, my managing editor, has the gentlest and friendliest kicks-in-the-butt imaginable. If there were an archetypical "creative director," Donna Lebrecht would be it. Many thanks for her friendship and, well, creative direction. Jesse Olson, my friend and coincidentally, my son, is a constant source of motivation to leave some of myself behind. My very favorite person to tell stories to is my daughter, Kya, whose giggles and hugs are like diamonds in my life. Finally, Penny Pennington, partner in crime, straight shooter and spiritual explorer, is a constant source of laughter and wonderful ideas. I owe her, and of course she won't let me forget it . . .

EARTH TEACH ME QUIET, AS THE GRASSES ARE STILL WITH NEW LIGHT.
EARTH TEACH ME SUFFERING, AS OLD STONES SUFFER WITH MEMORY.
EARTH TEACH ME HUMILITY, AS BLOSSOMS ARE HUMBLE WITH BEGINNING.
EARTH TEACH ME CARING, AS MOTHERS NURTURE THEIR YOUNG.
EARTH TEACH ME COURAGE, AS THE TREE WHICH STANDS ALONE.
EARTH TEACH ME LIMITATION, AS THE ANT WHICH CRAWLS ON THE GROUND.
EARTH TEACH ME FREEDOM, AS THE EAGLE WHICH SOARS IN THE SKY.
EARTH TEACH ME ACCEPTANCE, AS THE LEAVES WHICH DIE IN THE FALL.
EARTH TEACH ME RENEWAL, AS THE SEED WHICH RISES IN THE SPRING.
EARTH TEACH ME TO FORGET MYSELF, AS MELTED SNOW FORGETS ITS LIFE.
EARTH TEACH ME TO REMEMBER KINDNESS, AS DRY FIELDS WEEP WITH RAIN.

UTE PRAYER
BY NANCY WOOD

PREFACE

For me, there has always been a suspicion that science and spirit were not mutually exclusive. From the time that I was a little kid exploring caves and rivers, I have recollections of watching wild animals. But the memories are also filled with feelings about those animals, and a suspicion that the differences between these other species and myself were not as huge as it appeared at first glance.

I had a strong interest in wildlife, so I took the best avenue that my culture offered, the world of science. The academic requirements for an advanced degree in zoology demanded an objective approach to the watching of wild animals. I did the work required, but I had already been ruined. I had been a kid with feelings once, and every time I was outside, in the real world, the feelings came back.

A typical, but not isolated, example of my internal paradox came in the middle of the experiment with academia. I was crouched and camouflaged, being a "scientist" at the edge of a beaver pond.

For a class project, I was observing beaver social behavior from an objective distance. It was nearly dark. I watched with a notebook on my lap as a large beaver (number 1A according to my color-coded ear tags) swam directly at me. It came ashore, waddled over to my rubber-bottomed boots, sniffed them thoroughly, and deposited a squirt of castoreum (an anise-smelling musk) on the left boot. I was trying not to breathe, but at the same time my mind was racing with interpretations. Was this an act of disdain? Was I claimed as territorial property? For lack of anything else to say, I wrote "observer becomes participant" in the notebook.

It would have been a cop-out to say something like "territorial instinct" or "reaction to agitating stimulus." But deep down I knew that these phrases were all great-sounding euphemisms for "I don't know." In reality, I had just become a "recovering" biologist.

There were plenty of similar experiences, like imitating bird calls so the birds would land on my head, or watching coyotes kill a deer by means of an elaborate ruse. I began to see animals' actions as "talk," and my observations as "listening" to their language.

Gradually, I began to realize that my outdoor experiences were the same ones people had been having on this continent for twelve thousand years. I became interested in how *they* saw things. I encountered real people, people with strength and frailities, but also people with ancient, perfected traditions. On this continent, they were my Elders, with thousands of years of experience to offer.

This book is an outgrowth of the stories given to me by these Elders, Native Americans whose stories compelled a comparison of two worlds. These worlds seemed very different to me at first, until I remember that I was a kid once, and both were probably inside of me all along.

INTRODUCTION
GIVING VOICE

IT IS TRUE THAT MANY OF THE OLD WAYS HAVE BEEN LOST. BUT JUST AS THE RAINS RESTORE THE EARTH AFTER A DROUGHT, SO THE POWER OF THE GREAT MYSTERY WILL RESTORE THE WAY AND GIVE IT NEW LIFE. WE ASK THAT THIS HAPPEN NOT JUST FOR THE RED PEOPLE, BUT FOR ALL THE PEOPLE, THAT THEY ALL MIGHT LIVE. IN IGNORANCE AND CARELESSNESS THEY HAVE WALKED ON INA MAKA, OUR MOTHER. THEY DID NOT UNDERSTAND THAT THEY ARE PART OF ALL BEINGS, THE FOUR-LEGGED, THE WINGED, GRANDFATHER ROCK, THE TREE PEOPLE, AND OUR STAR BROTHERS. NOW OUR MOTHER AND ALL OUR RELATIONS ARE CRYING OUT. THEY CRY FOR THE HELP OF ALL PEOPLE.

LAKOTA PRAYER

Because it is impossible to pinpoint the personal philosophies of individuals, using the words "Native American" is a generalization which is convenient, but not necessarily clear. An Abenaki is not a Lakota is not a Tlingit. These are very different people in some ways, but very similar in others. Assuming that the different Native American Nations are equivalent to one another is like saying that all Swedes are like all Arabs. The *similarities* between Native Nations are the focus of this book. When I refer to "Native American," I refer only to a similar theme among *traditional* Native Americans. I would never presume to speak for an individual.

There are some Native American people who believe that personal power is at stake when our "stories" are given away. I think I know where that perception comes from. Five hundred years of taking by Europeans and their descendants would make anyone want to hold tightly to whatever is left. But I have also encountered elders who understand that the wisdom inside stories which if freely given can, by definition, *not* be stolen.

We are bounded by physical bodies and countless other limitations, but we are transcended by the stories we carry and pass to others, and by the risks we take in that process. We are not important. We are vessels carrying water in a desert and fire through a blizzard. Our importance lies in the thoughts we carry, and the sharing of water and fire with those who follow.

Don't get me wrong—I don't feel I have to "either-or" between the world of science and a world full of mystery. With the help of people who lived with the North American land for millennia, I have simply learned to remain open to possibilities. Real "science" is not just the realm of the learned and dogmatic. It is also compatible with being a learner, a student. It is a process of accepting—perhaps even being eager for—the hundred questions contained in each answer. Good students listen hard, and are not afraid to hear subtle pain inside of obvious anger, harsh reality inside of soft words, or the whimper in a war cry.

This book is about an opportunity. We have, to this point, looked at multi-cultural education as learning "about" other cultures. Because of our own world view, it hasn't occurred to us that we might learn "from" other cultures. Don't worry, I'm not talking about living in teepees and forsaking our technological advantages. This opportunity is about new ways to see, a perspective that has been hiding in plain sight since the beginnings of our interactions with the First Nations on this continent. Those who lived comfortably and sustainably on this land for twenty thousand years did so because of their world view, not because of their technological incompetence. Perhaps, if we are willing to put away fear and truly listen, they can teach us how to survive here for twenty thousand more.

This book is about Native American stories. For me, listening to these stories has been more than survival training. My ways of seeing my friends, my politics, my relationships with other beings and with "inanimate things" have been altered. An example of those internal differences is the broadening of my concept of time. "Indian Time" is no longer a way to explain the "laziness" of a people who has never made artificial marks on a dial and called it "real time." Time is a perception. We all know that one twenty-minute period will seem like a minute, and another will seem like a day. Native People simply acknowledged that perception. Their rhythms were the rhythms of the land. Those same "lazy" people worked twenty-four-hour days during the ricing season, the syrup season or the salmon run.

Of course, I also *see* stories differently. It is interesting how tainted our perception of stories has become. "Story," "myth," "fable," "tale"—all of these words have come to represent something we don't have to take very seriously. Yet, stories are perhaps the most uniquely "human" thing about us.

In western thought, stories are entertainment, a way to kill time until some important task comes our way. Native American stories have been thought of as "cute" tales of animals for the amusement of children. The western frame of reference is that of separation—the processes of nature are removed from the human world, fact is absolute, perception can be purified of bias, observers are different from participants.

In the Native world view, there are only participants—the act of observing is a form of participation. In this framework, there is no framework. Thoughts, feelings, actions and stories are interwoven in Nature, and *everything*, even the darkest secret feelings we tell no one else, has a set of consequences connected to it. It is no wonder that traditional Native people acted with such a sense of responsibility toward the land. They saw no difference between the land and themselves.

This view, of course, makes the land sacred, and ourselves simple and temporary expressions of the land. Property, a sacred institution in my own culture, is an artificial concept to a traditional Native American. Boundaries are, to them, invisible lines with no importance to birds, seeds or dragonflies. "Real estate" is an oxymoron.

Life becomes inclusive in the Native view. Everything is alive. "Beings" includes the soil and the stars. And most importantly, no individual is alive all by itself, in a vacuum. Science, perhaps unintentionally, supports this perspective. We completely replace the atoms in our bodies every seven years or so, making us "recycling processes" rather than separate individuals. Our molecules are recycled mastodon, trilobite and star dust. John Muir once said that everything is hitched to everything else in the universe, but he had it only half right. We are not only hitched to everything else, we are made of everything else.

This is a sobering idea for those who want to feel a sense of superiority over other expressions of life. Organized religion, politics, and economic systems are often based on the idea that we have dominion over everything else because of inherent supremacy. In another reality, this illusion only prevents us from seeing, let alone accepting, the unique gifts of other species. We *are* what we wish to dominate. . .

To many traditional Native Americans, this is arrogance and ignorance of unbelievable proportions. Instead of "boss/worker," "master/slave," "chosen few/peons," "ruler/subject"—all top-to-bottom arrangements of the world—they see everything on the same equal footing, even the human animal.

In the traditional Native world, the Great Mystery (God) is inside of, and moves through, all things—on the same plane. God is not "up there," with dozens of popes, cardinals, bishops, priests, gurus, and seers gaining their employment by standing between the Great Mystery and us. Rather, God is expressed by all of creation. Equally. A horizontal arrangement of the universe does not allow for arrogance or subservience. There is "other" power, but not "higher" power.

From the horizontal perspective, traditional Native Americans watched animals carefully. Their lives depended on the knowledge they gained from their observations. Most animals were endowed with certain traits of character, and the Natives tried to imitate the behaviors they admired, to form themselves in the image of those ideals. Note that the frame of reference for desired behavior was not the human animal. Humans were not thought to innately possess any of those desired traits—the characteristics were learned behaviors. In this way the traditional Native did not learn *about* animals, in the scientific sense, but learned *from* them how to live. There was no assumption, as in western society, that the animals were somehow inferior to two-leggeds. There were human people, bear people, tree people, rock people—all equally gifted with their own views of the world. They all reflected the future, fed each other, and taught each other.

The level of respect given to the rest of nature by aboriginal humans on every continent showed this same wisdom. Without any fossil record to guide them, there was still the correct assumption that the other "people" were our elders, and they should have the same respect as human elders, if not more. Success, in this case measured by the longevity of the species, was not up for argument. The "seniority system" was measured in millions of years. A hierarchy of "importance" had to be manufactured by western civilization, and drawn in biology books with humans at the apex of the evolutionary tree. The First Peoples on our continent had no such illusions.

Considering the struggles we are now having with our own environment, perhaps it is time to listen to some old teachers—the ones who have been here for eons. Native People aren't the original teachers. They simply listened to the rest of the Earth with an open heart, giving voice to bear, eagle, raven and stone, and carried the water through the desert, to us. In the next chapters, perhaps we can take a sip or two.

CHAPTER ONE

Coyote
THE DEVIL DIVINE

GRAY COYOTE IS A DIRTY MEDDLER,
HE WEARS A BELT OF SNAKE SKIN.

GRAY COYOTE STOOD IN THE FOREST,
FROM HIS SHOULDERS HE PLUCKED FEATHERS
THAT GAVE ME SHINING POWER,
PLUCKED WING FEATHERS BEARING POWER.

PIMA SONG

So, what is Coyote doing wearing feathers? Why would a dirty meddler be generous with power? And isn't divine devil an oxymoron?

Well, yes, Coyote *is* a living, breathing oxymoron. He is creator and destroyer, a trickster and a simpleton, a walking contradiction. He has a simple message: the world is full of paradox—get used to it.

The western scientific tradition has always seen any paradox, any mystery, as a "seeming" paradox and an "as-yet-unsolved" mystery. We demand an explanation, a reason, a logical deductive response to apparent contradictions. "What's the moral of the story?" is our response to a Native tale. If we can't find the moral, then we dismiss a story as pure entertainment, with no serious utilitarian purpose. "Lighten up," says Coyote.

"Controlling the variables" is one of the basic tenets of scientific inquiry. Control is the operative word in this principle. Coyote says, "Variables vary. That's their job—to be *out* of control." Most of what we call "control" amounts to wishful thinking, salve for a suppressed fear of the unknown. The classic Serenity Prayer speaks of "accepting the things we can not change." Coyote speaks of accepting the things we will never understand.

Attempts at creating an illusion of control in western culture are almost comical. We look at the capriciousness of nature and invent Murphy's "Law," a law which wryly admits that there are very few laws. Coyote and Murphy must have been good friends.

Coyote is random, bawdy, irreverent, foolish, inconsistent and destructive, a frightening package. If these qualities imply amoral anarchy and chaos, we have to remember Coyote's internal paradox—he is also the creative force to Native Americans in the universe. Coyote's misadventures get him and others into serious trouble sometimes. He often gets killed in the process of the story. But, life goes on. Coyote simply remakes himself out of some remnant of his former self, and moves to another story. Sometimes the only thing making sense in a coyote story is that life sometimes doesn't make sense.

Coyote is an embodiment of the things we cannot change or understand. Coyote must simply be accepted for who he is—analyzing him is a waste of time. Ultimately, Coyote, for all his infantile behavior, is about adulthood and maturity, an acceptance of human limitation. But he doesn't go further than that, into cynicism and powerlessness. Coyote also has the "courage to change the things he can." He takes constant risks, secure in the knowledge that the worst that could happen is he would move effortlessly into another story.

Coyote—beggar, thief, comic, philanderer, and role model. . .

There are more Coyote stories in Native lore than stories about any other creature. Many focus on Coyote's creative powers, in the form of original creation stories. Others focus on Coyote's jealousy of the names and qualities of other animals—he always wants to be able to do what other creatures can do, and those animals use that envy to their advantage. Considering Coyote's awesome and fickle powers, it is often a wise diversionary tactic to point out to Coyote some inane skill he does not possess. They will teach him. He always falls for it, because his ego is large and his discretion is tiny.

Creation is an overwhelming concept, considering the complexity of the world. There are equal amounts of life and death, pain and pleasure, happiness and sadness. The distribution of these elements has no "fairness" about it, so Coyote is the perfect model for a Creator. It is hard to say whether he gets credit or blame for creation, another contradiction with which Coyote would probably be comfortable.

A Crow story of creation starts with Coyote floating on a raft, on the endless sea. He is bored and alone, and decides to create some land. He calls to some ducks, a mallard, a canvasback and a pintail, to fetch him some mud from the bottom of the sea. They all fail, because they cannot dive deep enough. He then calls to the grebe, also called the mud hen, to get some mud. This, of course, is the sacred fourth attempt (patterns of four are found everywhere in Native teachings). Grebe brings some mud in its webbed foot.

Coyote then spreads the mud from the east to the south to the west to the north, creating the creatures. But first he waited for them to ask to be here. Wolf asked with a distant howl. Birds asked with their songs. The creatures willed themselves to be here. Coyote also made mountains, rivers and grasses. He formed the buffalo from some shiny black stones, and pulled a star from the sky to make sacred tobacco. That was how it all started.

The Nez Perce tell of the beginnings of humans. A giant white monster came down from the north and gobbled up all the small animals, sucking them in with its lungs. It then did the same to all the big animals too. Coyote, the only one left, was bored without all of his fellow creatures, and decided to challenge the monster to a fight. Coyote went to the top of the tallest mountain, made a rope and tied himself to the top of the mountain. From there he taunted the giant. The monster sucked until he was blue, but could not break the rope Coyote had made. The monster had power, but coyote was far smarter, and the monster was afraid. It decided to befriend Coyote, and invited him to stay in its cave.

Coyote talked to the monster for a long time, and when he was trusted by the giant he asked if he could go into its stomach to see the animals it had swallowed. The giant thought that this was a good idea and thought, "I don't have to swallow Coyote, he goes of his own will!" Coyote went in, but brought some sticks and a knife. Inside he told the other animals not to worry, and built a huge fire. The giant screamed and began to melt. Coyote reached up and cut out the heart of the beast. They all escaped.

Coyote wanted to celebrate his victory, so he cut the monster into four pieces and threw them to the four directions. They turned into the black, white, yellow, and red people of the world. From the blood in the butchering spot, he created the Nez Perce.

With fire and knives, the Native people of the north have kept winter in check since the time of the great glaciers—white monsters that came from the north and scattered the animals to the south. The story is not just a metaphor about the early times. It is also a reminder of *our* origins. The products of Coyote's celebration were human beings, but the raw materials tell of the monster just below the surface in all of us. Like Coyote, *just* like Coyote, we have contradictory sides. Good and evil may be clear in the movies, but those qualities become very fuzzy when we see ourselves reflected in the eyes of Coyote.

The Klikitat have a very similar story of Coyote slaying a monster and retrieving the animal people from inside it. The only significant difference is that the Klikitat people related the story to where they live north of the Columbia River. The Columbia becomes a violent river where it forces itself through the Cascade Range. The Monster lived along the river and ate the animals as they attempted to travel in their canoes. From that place in the story, Coyote kills the monster in exactly the same way as in the Nez Perce story, and names the animals as they emerge. He strikes a deal with the monster's spirit. It must live beneath the river and take one of the new animals, the humans, only once in a while, leaving the rest alone.

Today, the monster has transformed. It takes the form of eleven monster-sized dams on the Columbia River, and eats far more salmon and steelhead than the agreement called for. It may be headed for another confrontation with Coyote. . .

Coyote is irreverent at the peril of everyone else. The consequences of his arrogance are rarely paid by Coyote himself. Some animals are just in the wrong place at the wrong time. A Shoshone story tells of Coyote walking right up to and spitting on a sacred white rock, which everyone else was afraid of. The rock began to roll after Coyote, who ran through streams, up hills, through gorges—and still the rock was right behind. Coyote tricked an elk and a bear into jumping in front of the rock. It just crushed them and kept on rolling closer to Coyote.

A human, who was building a fire, heard coyote go past, whimpering. He stuck out his elbow, which had beads wrapped around it, and smashed the rock into tiny pieces. Coyote, being Coyote, was grateful only for a few seconds, but then killed the man and took the beads. He went around smashing larger and larger rocks. He was about to smash the largest rock, but the rock was quicker and crushed him. Only a tail showed where Coyote used to be.

One of the most common stories all across western North America has Coyote learning to use eyes from a human, a chickadee or some other animal. Depending on the story's origin, Coyote goes through various misadventures and loses his eyes. He sometimes gets them back by posing

as another animal. Or he "borrows" an eye from a buffalo and another from a mouse, and then he must walk holding his head to the side to keep the eyes from rolling out.

Giving up old eyes, or seeing with new ones, is a common theme in Native stories. To do either, a person must take an extreme risk, or at least blunder into the new condition while having fun. Coyote is the model, constantly asking the rhetorical question, "What's the worst that could happen?"

An Assiniboine story recalls a kind of trouble Coyote had under his tail. He was trotting along on the prairie when a very quiet voice said, "We are the strongest people in the world. . ."

"Who was that?" Coyote demanded.

"We are the strongest people in the world. . ." something whispered, down low.

Coyote put his ear down close to the ground.

"We are the strongest people in the world. . ." It was the Grass People!

"Hah!" Coyote said. "I'll show you Grasses who is strongest!" He ate them. All of them.

Coyote trotted off again. A little while later, the voice came back, even quieter than before. "We are the strongest people in the world. . ." his stomach hummed.

"Quiet!" Coyote barked. But his stomach talked louder and louder and it grew like a balloon.

Just then, all of the songs of the Grasses in Coyote's stomach came out. Boom! He broke wind. Coyote was thrown far into the sky by the force. He landed hard. A big knot grew on his head. Boom! This time, even farther into the sky! Coyote broke bones this time.

"Hah! I'm still alive!" he taunted the Grasses.

BOOM! Coyote went so high into the air he was flattened when he landed. Dead.

His bones bleached out in the sun and wind, and the Grasses re-planted themselves. One day fox came by and picked up a leg bone. Fox tossed it into the air, playing, and it turned back into Coyote. He yawned after his long sleep and trotted off across the prairie.

Coyote is probably doomed to repeat the same mistake someday. We seem to have this recurrent moral crisis in our culture, too. The food chain,

starting with the plants which convert sunlight to stored energy, is constant and immutable. Life can get along without coyotes and humans, probably, but not without plants. We must learn about our own vulnerability over and over, it seems.

In the early times, according to the Caddo People, there was no death. Everything which had been created stayed here, and soon the world became very crowded. The chiefs of all the animals got together and agreed that everyone should die for a short time and then come back to life. Coyote disagreed, saying that the world would still keep getting more crowded, only at a slower rate. He was outvoted, so the chiefs built a special grass lodge facing east. When the first animal died, a human, the body was placed in the lodge. The medicine chiefs began to sing a renewal song. A whirlwind blew in from the west, circled the lodge, and paused by the door. Coyote streaked in from a hidden spot and slammed the door shut. The whirlwind blew away, and since that time death has been forever.

Coyote was frightened about sabotaging the will of the other chiefs, and to this day slinks across the prairie, constantly looking back over his shoulder for whirlwinds or angry animals.

In this case, Coyote was wiser than we are. We still fight against the idea of death, but Coyote knew that life should exist at the edge of death, and that life and death should feed each other. They are both essential, whether we like the idea or not. Once again, Coyote's lesson comes home. Accept the things you cannot change or control. His life reminds us that paradox need not be too complicated. His ironic message is: the way to happiness is to be happy. It is nothing more than a simple choice.

CHAPTER TWO

Raven
WING-STROKES OF GENIUS

I ARISE FROM REST WITH MOVEMENTS
SWIFT AS THE BEAT OF RAVEN WINGS.
I ARISE TO MEET THE DAY,
HOUA. HOUA.
MY FACE IS TURNED FROM THE DARK OF NIGHT
TO GAZE AT THE DAWN OF DAY
NOW LIGHTENING THE SKY.

INUIT SONG

Coyote's counterpart in northwestern North America, from the Oregon coast to the north slope of Alaska, is Raven. He is creator and trickster, deity and clown, caretaker and mischief-maker, just like Coyote. In the distant time, according to Koyukon tradition, Raven saved the world from darkness. There was a woman who stole the sun and kept it rolled in a blanket in her lodge. Raven, the trickster, changed himself into a spruce needle so he could be swallowed by the woman. Raven made the woman pregnant, and was born as a son. When he became old enough to play, Raven the creator rolled the sun out the door and followed it. He flew the sun up into the sky to light up the world. The sun was heavy, so Raven had to beat his wings loudly to get into the air. His wings are still loud today.

Ravens function as opportunistic scavengers in nature. They are expert at tricking wolves, foxes, eagles, wolverines and even grizzly bears out of part of their hard-earned food. So distasteful are the habits of Raven, that the northern forest natives swear he sleeps under a dog skin, one of the foulest things anyone can do. Yet Raven is treated with respect because of his power and relative benevolence. He is the rogue with the good heart beneath. He created a perfect world at the beginning, but made it imperfect later. The world was more interesting that way. As an example, Raven changed the rivers, which once flowed two ways, depending on which side of the stream a person floated. They now flow only one way, because it is more fun to watch humans struggle upstream.

In the eastern woodlands of this continent, the trickster-creator character is the Hare. The Ojibwe of the north woods have Maymaygwaysi, the little hairy-faced gnome who lives in the cracks of rocks close to the water. There is probably a similar character for every aboriginal culture on the planet. Life is unpredictable everywhere, and we all need some way of coping with that—or at least someone to blame.

Not only are characters similar worldwide, but some stories are too. One in particular probably originated about 9,000 years ago when the great continental glaciers melted and raised sea level by 300 feet—a flood by anyone's standards. The Tlingit, Kwakiutl, and inland Koyukon tell (with some variation) about Raven making a huge raft and putting pairs of animals on the raft until the flood waters went away. All the humans were killed in the flood, so Raven had to make humans again.

Sound familiar? Geologists have their own deluge story—less metaphorical perhaps, but still very similar. An interesting difference between the old world/biblical versions and the new world concerns the time of the appearance of humans. Humans built the boat in the old world, but they are invented or reinvented after the flood here. Even this discrepancy could have a corollary in the scientific view. Humans are recent arrivals

on this continent. In fact, most archeologists time the arrival during the last gasp of the glaciers, just before the flood. Hey, Raven knows what he is doing. . .

The capriciousness of Raven is a not-so-subtle reminder of the mysterious ways of natural process. Western European tradition has a lot of trouble with mysteries. They are always "solved" at the end of the book, movie or mini-series. Raven, and his counterparts, remind us that mystery is perfectly normal. Traditional Native people do not have a single centralized God in the monarchical tradition (usually modeled after a male human). There is spirit in everything, and therefore God in everything. When we look at a grasshopper as a manifestation of God, it profoundly changes our relationship and sense of responsibility to the grasshopper. This kind of "God in all" view extended to the Rock People, the Cloud People, and all the other "inanimate" but essential parts of nature. In other words, God can not be put in a convenient box, such as many religions do by personifying and deifying a human. Native people correctly saw that this would soon turn into a license to abuse the other species and elements of creation. God may have created us, but *we* created God "in our image." Traditional Native people had no such arrogance. They were much more honest about what they did not know. There is simply a Great Mystery which moves through all things. They make no silly attempts to explain the unexplainable.

Raven is an obvious reminder that divisions between good and evil, thing and process, God and creation are arbitrary. Just when you think you have it figured out, Raven teaches otherwise.

The interchangeability of Raven's sides, and the unpredictability of his actions, become admonitions to be careful in our everyday actions—you can never completely predict the consequences. In fact, unless a person carefully considers the results of his or her actions on their own seventh generation (and all those in between), the results could be immediate. Raven constantly gets himself into trouble by not considering consequences. When we mess around with nature for short-term personal gain, the immediate result may be "scientifically uncertain," but there is damage to our spirits because we even *considered* acting without full knowledge of the consequences. What kind of person has this made me, to myself and to my children, is the important question. Raven acts selfishly, and pays.

The kind of reciprocal relationship a person has with nature if he or she believes in control is "I take, therefore I get." It gives us a unilateral "right" to exploit what we call "natural resources," a name which implies that nature becomes valuable when it has value to *us*. We feel we can modify the consequences later. The Native view is diametrically opposed. A Native would reason, "I sacrifice, therefore I will likely benefit." Native people often would give away everything they had in their possession, secure that (a) they never "owned" anything anyway and (b) the real reward was internal peace, not external goods. Sounds a lot more Christian than most of Christianity, doesn't it?

Raven, in a Tlingit story, deals with selfishness and hoarding in a story that should probably be told at every water rights conference. Old man Petrel had a beautiful freshwater spring in his lodge. It was the only one in existence, and no one else could use the water. The other animals were very thirsty, and called on Raven to do something with his powers to help. Raven, who was white back then, went to the door of Petrel and began to tell hilarious stories about his misadventures. Petrel invited him in to hear more stories, but Raven had so many that Petrel eventually fell asleep. Raven then took out some rotten moss and placed it under Petrel on his blanket. Petrel woke up and was convinced he had lost bowel control in his sleep. He grabbed some water in a skin and went outside to wash the blanket. Raven had a big mouth (obviously), and he swallowed most of the spring water. Petrel came in and caught him in the act. Raven flew up to the smoke hole and got stuck—he was too full of water. Petrel started a fire under Raven and the smoke turned him black. Raven spat out some of the water and put out the fire. The water he spat was just enough to allow him to escape. As he flew away, he dribbled water all over the Northwest, making rivers, streams and lakes everywhere. Today Petrel is a sea bird which rarely comes close to fresh water.

Selfishness has had long-term consequences to Petrel—he must do without the very thing which he hoarded. It is interesting that the concept of pollution (fouling his own nest) was so closely associated with keeping all of a natural thing for one's self. If Petrel is not a metaphor for western civilization, which believes in the divine right of humans to own the earth, I would be very surprised.

Raven, in his own tradition, is sometimes on the other side of the moral fence. A Haida, Tahltan and Bella Coola tale tells of Raven's greed. He floated up a river in his boat, which was packed with just enough provisions for his journey, to a lodge. The inhabitants were only shadows, but they invited Raven in to share some fish and deer fat. Raven was afraid at first, but accepted the offer and went inside. They had boxes of food everywhere. He ate until he was full, and went back to his boat. He thought it would be a shame to waste all that good food on shadows, so he went back to steal the boxes. What could shadows do to him anyway?

They caught Raven stealing the boxes and beat him until he couldn't move. He crawled back to the boat and found it was empty, too. His beak is still swollen today from the beating.

This story is a reminder of those situations when we are all alone, with only ourselves (our shadow) to answer to, and an ethical problem presents itself to us. What will we do? Pretend that there are no consequences, or

understand that the results of our secret actions reach further than we can ever imagine? Which Raven are we like?

There are, of course, some Ravens we wouldn't care to emulate. Another Koyukon legend from the distant time tells of Raven when he lived with Mink. This was a great arrangement for Raven because, as usual, he didn't have to catch his own food. (To this day, ravens rarely kill their own food. They prefer to scavenge.) He ate the fish which Mink stored along the shore. Raven became bored with a constant diet of fish, so he convinced Mink to kill a bear for them both. Raven hid Mink inside a fish, and when the bear swallowed the fish, Mink came out and slashed the bear's insides and killed it. They ate well.

The deal Raven had made with Mink was that they would take turns hiding in the fish and killing bears. Raven was reluctant, but he eventually crawled inside the fish. A bear came by and was reaching for the fish when Raven squawked and jumped out, then flew away.

In real life, Raven shows more bravery. On a kill, ravens often show no fear of wolves, grizzlies, or wolverines. The big predators also seem to accept the raven's presence. Ravens can't eat much, so they are probably more of a help than a hindrance—they have sharp eyes, and will warn the wolves and bears when someone else approaches.

Humans tend to rush to judgment about animals that don't seem to have an obvious "purpose." Raven's story about cooperation with Mink points out the necessity of every living thing in the larger scheme. In a real sense, everything is symbiotic to everything else in nature. In the Native perspective it can be safely assumed that everything is essential to make the world work. Science grudgingly makes discovery after discovery which backs this view. "Parasites," we are learning, have more benefit to their unwilling hosts than we suspected. Leeches, for example, are now standard treatment for re-attaching human limbs after accidental amputation. Ten years ago they were universally cursed as useless and disgusting.

Raven often talks someone else into the dirty work, as in a Tsimshian and Nootka story about the arrival of fire. The fire lived out on a distant island. Raven convinced many different animals to try to bring the fire to him. Most of them failed, but Deer swam out and came back with the fire. (Deer have hollow hairs and float very high in the water.) Deer tied the fire to its tail, and it burned, turning the Deer into the black-tailed deer. Raven put some of the fire into flint stones from the beach. The fire comes out when the stones are struck with steel.

The Tsimshian also credit, or blame, Raven for the finite life span of humans. He walked into an argument between Stone and Elderberry over who would have their child first. Stone wanted to bet, "If I have my child first, humans will live a very long time, like me. If you are first, they will live a short time, like you."

Raven fixed the contest—he didn't like the idea of too many human children around. He touched Elderberry and she had her child first. To this day, elderberries grow from the graves of the people.

Raven often shirked his responsibilities, but when a difficult decision had to be made, he was there. We are in Raven's feathered robe these days. We can take our responsibilities toward the natural world seriously, or we can shrug our black shoulders and pretend we have an unlimited license to economic gain. We can steal from our own shadows, or we can understand that the shadows are extensions of ourselves.

29

CHAPTER THREE

Mouse
THE HUMBLE PATHFINDER

MOUSE,
WINGS OF BIRDS INVISIBLE,
ARE NOW FLUTTERING ABOVE YOU.
YOU STAND WITH FACE UPLIFTED.
AND QUIETLY LISTEN THERE.

OUR LAND WAS UNFORTUNATE.
THE FLOODS CAME ROLLING WESTWARD,
THEY CAME FLOWING WESTWARD,
AND I CRIED OUT MUCH AFRAID.

PIMA FLOOD CYCLE SONG

Native Americans must have felt like the humble Mouse in the face of a flood of white men who rolled westward across the land. Despite the fact that they were defending their homes, the Native people were severely disadvantaged in this war for two reasons. Whites had great technological and numerical advantage—cannons and Gatling guns, for example. The other disadvantage was psychological.

Natives were, by nature, humble. The concept of "superiority" was completely alien to their world view. Before the white men came, there were strict rules of engagement in war. No one had a "right" to do what they wished because they felt superior to the enemy. The "all's fair in war" doctrine made the invaders ruthless beyond belief to Native Americans. When, for ten thousand years, a people has made a point of being *no* better than any other part of creation, the idea of manifest destiny made no ethical sense. Honor seemed to be only worth the paper it was printed on. Because they did not adjust to this strange way of thinking, Native Americans lost the war, for the time being.

But despite the conventional wisdom of their cultures, people like Ghandi, Jesus, Chief Seattle, Siddhartha, and St. Francis—who would be eaten alive in today's western society—were more humble than their followers. They left a permanent legacy, and their contributions continue to shape the earth in positive ways.

Traditional Native people see notoriety as a weakness, an attempt to fill a hungry and empty heart with fluff. The heart is filled from within, not with the outside approval of other empty hearts. Mouse, the quiet, tiny secretive animal, is the model for the amount of hubris which is appropriate in everyday life. Equality is a basic assumption, and it extends into the non-human world as well.

Our dominant culture thinks vertically. God-Pope-Cardinal-Archbishop. . . down to the lowly sinner. King-Queen-Archduke. . . to the peons. President-Vice President-Speaker-Senator-Congressman. . . down to those who pay their bills. Star-producer-director. . . down to the key grips and moviegoers. For a society which professes that "all men are created equal," we have a lot of assumed inequality. Nearly everything is arranged vertically, with a highest and lowest, a most important and least important.

Native American tradition does not even accept the idea of hierarchies, let alone construct them. They see similarities among us, not differences. Every stone and ant and plant is a teacher, an expert at something, and we are the students. For this reason, they watched each other, and the rest of the world, carefully. Among Natives, every person in the village had a specific and equally important role to play in everyday life. A chief or a shaman was not better than everyone else because of his position. He was only the best *in that role*.

Without hierarchies, the world becomes horizontal, at least in the figurative sense. God becomes the Great Mystery which moves equally through all things. A stone is as important, in the overall scheme of things, as a human. This concept rankles the human race, who are used to getting their way with the world. Accepting real equality demands considerable shrinking of the human ego. Enter the teacher, Mouse.

In the last few hundred years, most of the Plains Native Americans have lived by the "medicine wheel" belief system. There are many regional variations on the theme, but in general, it concerns the cyclic nature of things and a quest for balance in the desirable attributes of an individual. The visual representation of these things is a wheel, representing the circular character of the universe, with four spokes, representing the four cardinal directions. Ceremonies having to do with the medicine wheel concept are usually begun in an easterly direction, and move "sunwise" to the south, west and north, in that order. Each direction represents a number of philosophical ideals, and has a totem animal and a symbolic color for that direction.

East is the dawning of any new day or experience (and thus most ceremonies begin facing that direction). The color of the new sun is gold, and the totem animal is usually the golden eagle, representing clear vision outside ourselves. To see the outer world clearly is to have the qualities of the eagle.

In the south, where the warmth of the midday sun and the summer comes from, the representative color is green, for the growth of new parts of our experience. To Natives, who were the keenest observers of nature, no animal represented exploration and discovery better than the mouse. Constantly scurrying under leaves and grasses to find new roots or berries or holes, the mouse was the explorer, expanding a tiny world to far horizons.

The west, where the sun disappears into the edge of the world and brings the black of night, was represented by the bear. Bear is the model of introspection, of looking within. Because the bear spends its waking hours in the dark and its sleeping hours in the depth of a den, it has ample opportunity to look at itself carefully.

Winter is the time of dormancy and renewal. The white snows come from the north, and are carried by the wolf in the woodland or the buffalo on the prairie. These animals represent knowledge and intelligence.

The four directions come together in the center, or hub, of the wheel.

This is the place of balance, where a person can know many things, like the wolf, but not forget how to explore and discover new things, like the mouse. In the center, our ability to see the world clearly, like the eagle, is balanced by our ability to look within, like the bear. The center of the wheel is where we are securely tied to our Mother, the earth, and where our spirits can fly with our Father, the sky. Physically, the wheel often has tie-down cords and a feather at the hub.

The humble exploration of the mouse is captured in a story first recorded by Hymeyohsts Storm, a Northern Cheyenne teacher. It tells of a Mouse who lived by a river. This Mouse explored for food near his home, but was intrigued by stories of the Sacred Mountain which the elders told. One day he decided to find the Sacred Mountain for himself.

He set out along the river and floated across on a large leaf with the help of a frog, who named him Jumping Mouse. On the other side he found a fat mouse with no interest in going anywhere else. The fat mouse was found and eaten by a snake. Jumping Mouse found a blind buffalo on the prairie. The buffalo was such a great animal, Jumping Mouse felt that he should have his eyes. The buffalo was so grateful for the gift, it led blind Jumping Mouse to the foot of the Sacred Mountain. There he found a wolf who could no longer smell. Such a great animal should have a good nose, thought Jumping Mouse, so he gave his nose to the wolf. The wolf led Jumping Mouse near the peak of the Sacred Mountain, but the Mouse could not see or smell anything. The wolf reassured Jumping Mouse and told him to accept the magic of the Mountain, even if it was frightening. Just then a dark shadow cooled the back of Jumping Mouse and something let out a blood-curdling scream. The Mouse was scared. He felt a sharp pain in his back, but then the pain went away and he felt light, almost weightless. His eyes began to see some blurry light and he saw the earth moving far below. Soon the world became crystal clear, and Jumping Mouse realized he was flying.

"You have a new name!" called the wolf, from far below. "You are Eagle."

The story of Jumping Mouse is a lesson in humility, sacrifice, risk and exploration, overcoming fear, and perseverance. Humility creates an interesting paradox—the humble teacher doesn't realize he or she is a teacher. A teacher who teaches with deeds, by example, simply lives life while the students watch.

Coyote once managed to get himself in trouble with mice. A Blackfoot story tells about the time Coyote heard a commotion inside of an elk skull. He put his eye down close and saw that the mice were having a dance. The Mouse Chief started the dance by chanting about mice winking their eyes. Then they all danced in a circle. Coyote, of course, is always envious of anyone's enjoyment, so he asked the chief if he could join in the dance. The chief pointed out that Coyote was too big to fit in the skull, but perhaps he could just stick his head inside. He warned Coyote that the rule of the mice was that they dance all night, and he

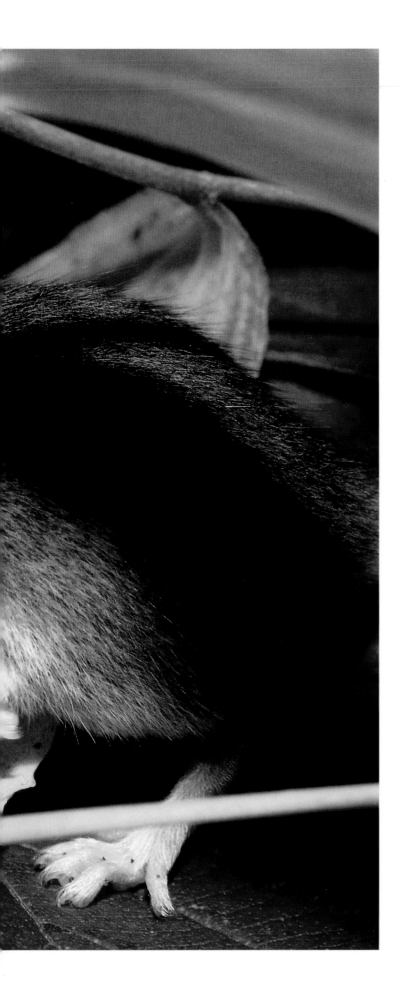

made Coyote promise to stay awake. Coyote, being Coyote, fell asleep.

The mice cut all the hair off his sleeping head, and his head swelled and was stuck in the skull. The mice were gone when he woke up, and because he couldn't see, he fell into the river and wandered into a camp of humans. They thought he was an elk, and an old woman crushed the elk skull with a big rock. When Coyote's bare head showed, the old woman hit him many more times because she was afraid of the strange bare-headed animal. Coyote went home with a huge headache. Coyote paid for not honoring the customs of those who gave him the gift of the dance.

The essence of leadership is service to those who are led. Mouse is not a leader because of some declaration. His humility, generosity and innocence are inseparable—they are the products of one another. Mice are small, nocturnal and hard to find. Humility is hard to find, too. If we look hard for the Mouse inside, we may discover a true warrior beneath our insecurities.

CHAPTER FOUR

Bear
The Wild Within

I AM LIKE A BEAR.
I HOLD UP MY HANDS
WAITING FOR THE SUN TO RISE.

NORTHERN UTE SONG

We are all like bears. We are omnivores, and eat a wide variety of foods. So do bears. We walk on two legs. So do bears sometimes. Bears, without their hair, look eerily like a human. We both can be secretive or fierce, introspective or curious about the world outside ourselves. We both demand respect from the other creatures because of our power.

To Native people, bears *are* us, or at least part of us. That wild, untamable side of us is the part that becomes the bear, when we let it. Bears put on the intellectual skins of humans and walk among us. We put on the emotional skins of bears and disappear into the dark mystery of the forest. So awesome is the bear, so unmentionable the wild side of the human, that many Native people do not, from respect, ever address the bear directly by name. The "dark thing" over there (Haida), the "unmentionable big animal" (Blackfoot), the "one going around the woods" (Tlingit), the "four-legged human" (Cree)—all are terms of respect and honor, usually preceded by an expression of relationship like "Brother" or "Grandfather."

In the great medicine wheel of the Native Plains people, bears—nocturnal, nearsighted, solitary, staying in a cave for half the year—are the keepers of the west, where the sun disappears and gives way to the darkness. This is the place of introspection, of "looking within." The bear is the model for knowledge of self as a source of power.

Sleeping for the winter in a dark place has long been a model for transformation. The bear that emerges in the spring is different from the bear that disappeared in the fall. People in the Southwest built dark meditative rooms with a small hole in the top as the entrance, called kivas. The human that emerges from the kiva after a few days is certainly different from the human that entered it. The result of looking carefully at ourselves, without distractions, is always transforming. Understanding the landscape within is key to understanding the landscape outside ourselves. We "see" and "hear" in a unique way, based on our *perspective,* but without careful focus on our inner selves, this perspective is often lost in the chaos of everyday existence, and we rely on others to tell us what our own perspective is. The bear knows this, and shows us a way to operate from the center of ourselves.

Native American stories of bears are told in two basic forms, and sometimes they are a combination of the two. In one form, a woman becomes mated to a bear, and in the other, a bear is killed with great ceremony. Often the "transformation" represented by the bear den is death. The bear and the human are interchangeable, and death is only a metamorphosis to another side of ourselves.

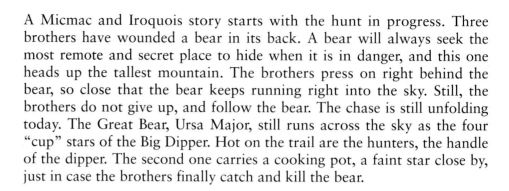

A Micmac and Iroquois story starts with the hunt in progress. Three brothers have wounded a bear in its back. A bear will always seek the most remote and secret place to hide when it is in danger, and this one heads up the tallest mountain. The brothers press on right behind the bear, so close that the bear keeps running right into the sky. Still, the brothers do not give up, and follow the bear. The chase is still unfolding today. The Great Bear, Ursa Major, still runs across the sky as the four "cup" stars of the Big Dipper. Hot on the trail are the hunters, the handle of the dipper. The second one carries a cooking pot, a faint star close by, just in case the brothers finally catch and kill the bear.

This story is still developing. Every autumn, when the sun has set, the Great Bear runs upside down across the sky. The wound on its back spills blood, turning the leaves red on the land below.

This is more than a cute way of explaining a constellation, because it also says important things about stories, and our relationships with the things around us. Few Native stories are linear, with a beginning and an end. Usually, some aspect of the story moves smoothly into the present day—the story is not completely resolved. In the Western European tradition, linear time is marked with "progress," a concept based entirely on an ever-increasing material wealth. Politicians constantly remind us to ask ourselves "Are we better off than we were before?" but the intent of the rhetorical question is seldom a call to measure our progress in spiritual growth or wisdom.

Native Americans see time as cyclic—themes unravel over and over again, without a definite beginning or ending. The outward appearance of the world may change. We may put satellites into the sky, build ever more powerful computers, put three chickens in every pot and four cars in the garage—but the real essence of humanity demands a cycle, a recurrent moral crisis which we must transcend to become more human, and more bear. Stories are never "done." They wait to include us, and for us to carry them with our words. Some day, perhaps, the bear and hunters will come back to this world with something they have learned and wish to share with us. The story leaves open the possibility.

One of the constant transformations humans undergo is a developmental passage from one world into another. Cultures must first recognize that these passages exist—such as childhood to adulthood—and then design rites to ease the transition. The "primitive" cultures on this planet have done a far more thorough job identifying and addressing these passages. A son "dies" to his mother (representing the childhood need for nurturing) and is reborn to the adult world. Some Native nations have bear rituals in their initiation rites. They dance a bear hunt, "kill" the bear (to prove their worthiness), sleep in its den, and are reborn as a bear—a fierce and capable warrior. When they hunt the bear, they are hunting for themselves.

The sense of adventure in this kind of living story eases some of the emotional pain of puberty, and celebrates the change a young person must undergo. The trauma of adolescence is often ignored in the dominant western culture. Our children feel lost, without any validation for their own life processes, and we wonder why. Bears are only one of the hundreds of teachers available to us.

Trips into the "underworld" of the bear den also recognize the renewal qualities of the earth and the soil. Biologically, lowly dirt, humble humus, is where death is recycled back into life. Earth is, literally, the mother of us all. The requirements of status as a shaman in most cultures include dying to the old self—sometimes a literal near-death experience and sometimes a metaphorical death. Many a shaman has emerged from a bear den with a bear guardian.

In the Cree tradition, a boy was once found and raised by a bear. The boy's human father never gave up hope of finding the lost son. He finally suspected that a bear may have captured the boy and began to hunt the bear. This was a hunt based on the power of individual spirits—hunter and bear each sang their own songs to see which was the most powerful. The wild side and the human side struggled for the spirit of the boy. The human father won, and killed the bear, but he realized that there was value to the "bear" side of the boy and wrapped one of the legs of the bear as a "gift" for the boy. The son kept the gift, and became the best bear hunter anyone could remember. A woman of the tribe became jealous of the young man's accomplishments, and wanted her own son to be the best hunter. She unwrapped the bear leg, but the gift of hunting skill was not transferable to anyone else—the son had *lived* with a bear, after all. Immediately, the young man turned into a bear and disappeared into the forest. The village never knew that kind of affluence again.

There are obvious morals in this story—about the uniqueness of gifts, about the usefulness of retaining an appropriate part of our past, and of the wild part of maleness. It speaks of jealousy and of the desirability of the "wild side" to women. And, of course, it speaks of looking a "gift bear" in the mouth.

Most of the woodland people, including the Ojibwe, Cree, Sauk, Fox, and Micmac, have a story about the importance of keeping *both* sides of ourselves. A pregnant woman, carrying twins, was killed by a horrible monster. One of the twins, Lodge-Boy, stumbled into a village and was raised by humans. The other was thrown into the woods by the monster and was found and raised by bears. Throw-Away-Boy was caught one day by the villagers, and reunited with his brother. Together, they had enough power to hunt and kill the monster.

Both Lodge-Boy, the reasoning human, and Throw-Away-Boy, the emotional and creative one, were necessary to the balance. Life's monsters, whether psychological or spiritual, can only be defeated with a balanced, whole person. We are only beginning to learn these ten-thousand-year-old lessons, and we still learn them the hard way.

One day, an Inuit woman was out berry-picking. (Berry-picking is often the beginning of a real-life encounter with a bear, so many bear stories open this way.) She picked her way farther and farther from the village until she was near the cave of a bear. She went inside and was killed by the resident. She was also pregnant with a son, whom the bear found as he was eating the woman. The bear was enamored with this boy, and raised him as his own son. The bear kept the secret of this boy's origins from him, but the son became interested in a skull he found on the cave floor. He played with it more and more, and as he did, he ranged farther and farther from the den. One day he met some two-leggeds. The shaman among them took some dust and formed the skull back into the boy's human mother.

Once again, the son can only be reunited with his mother after becoming initiated into the clan of the bear. In this case, the reconciliation between the genders demands an acceptance of differences, even if they are poorly understood by the other sex.

Another important transformation happens when a woman leaves her family of origin to marry a stranger. Her loyalties change. She becomes distant and unknown to her family, and also must place her trust in a frightening, powerful alien, the man she marries.

The Blackfoot people tell of a woman who went berry-picking into the mountains wearing a bear skin. There she was enchanted by a bear-man, and followed him to his cave. Even though he was massive and commanding he reassured her by gently removing a bone comb from her hair and speaking softly. They made love, delicately and wildly, and she decided to stay with this bear-man. The villagers searched for her, and called out to the bear to come down and fight. Bear-Skin-Woman begged

44

him to stay, but he told her he must go, to honor an old agreement between the humans and the bears. He was killed.

The people honored the bear by ritually and carefully cutting the meat in the woods, and eating him entirely—their part of the bargain. The woman came out of the cave and searched for some sign of her mate. She found a tiny piece of fat the people had overlooked, which she washed carefully and put under her dress. In her grief, she changed into a bear and killed some of the villagers so quickly they did not have time to react. She disappeared into the forest.

When her grieving time was over, she changed back into a kind woman who took care of her relatives. One day she was gathering cactus to feed everyone and the sharp needles poked her until she became pained and angry. Again, in her pain, she changed to a bear and marauded the village once more. Her nephews shot arrows at her and missed, all except the youngest. His arrow pushed her out of the camp. Still she did not give up, and attacked again. The youngest nephew used a magic feather to build obstacles in front of the bear, but finally had to climb a tree with his brothers. Realizing that the bear was too powerful, he shot his brothers with the arrows, pushing them into the sky. They became stars. He then tricked the bear into climbing the tree and shot the bear into the sky. The Great Bear chases the nephews (instead of the other way around) across the sky today.

The story has the obvious message about in-laws meddling in a marriage, and about innocence and youth sometimes being the only salvation of a people. But it is also a story about not trying to go back to a different time. People change—and the old familiar person will never be completely back. Times of grief, pain and anger remind us that we only keep our ideal person as an image in our minds, and only during the easy times. To struggle with pain or grief, to resist anger, is to call it down on ourselves. It sometimes works well to let the anger and pain go—to let the raging bear pass through the village without a power struggle.

In Blackfoot tradition, Bear-Skin-Woman has come back only once, bringing a medicine bundle and a pipe as an offering of a tenuous truce. When the pipe is smoked in a Blackfoot home, it is held with both hands, as a bear would hold it, in honor of the woman who married the bear.

Bears are so close to human form, they sometimes can seduce us from the boredom of everyday existence. An Ojibwe tale about a couple who took each other for granted teaches this lesson. They both wished for more passion in their relationship. The husband was more interested in hunting than in his wife. Even though he had plenty of dried meat for the winter, he insisted on going out again and again. His wife needed something to do, and decided to take two baskets into the forest, to pick blackberries. She went up the mountain and filled her baskets, but by the middle of the day had become hot and tired. She found a path, which seemed to go down the mountain, and followed it to a small opening in the forest. There, she lay down for a nap, spreading her hair in a fan on the grass. She dreamed of entering the forest and meeting a powerful young man with black hair. He reached out to touch her, and her clothes fell away. When they made love, it was fire and desire.

She woke up with a strange feeling, and saw two dark stains on the grass where the blackberry baskets were sitting. The blackberries had become juicy and soft. She walked toward home on the path, rounded a corner and met a bear. She slowly placed the baskets on the ground and stepped backward, but the bear wanted her, not the berries. She was frightened, and did not want to be eaten, so she used the only weapon she had, a beautiful song of praise for the bear. Slowly the bear began to relax, but every time she tried to edge past the bear it became wary and alert. She had to get closer and closer to the bear with her song. She reached out and touched the bear on its fur. The bear reached out and touched her gently, and her clothes fell away. Between them, it was fire, just like the dream. She happily gave the bear most of the berries, and returned home.

Every day she went back up the mountain, to gather the last berries of the season, she told her husband. Every day she returned with only a few berries in the basket, and she walked with more contentment and grace. Her husband was suspicious, and followed her one day to that place on the path. He was angry at what he witnessed, and pretended to be sick the next day, asking his wife to go fetch something very far from their house. While she was gone he dressed like a woman, met the bear on the path and killed it after a great battle. He was wounded in the fight, but managed to eat the bear's genitals and struggle home. His wife returned late that evening and gently washed his wounds. He reached out to touch her and her clothes fell away. They made love with more fire than they ever had.

He was still angry, and took her to see what was left of her bear lover. She screamed and grieved the bear, and immediately turned into a female bear and ran into the forest. She came back four nights to the lodge, but each time turned back into the forest. On some nights, there are beings walking the edge of the camp, just out of the fire light. Bearwalkers, they are called, sometimes wearing smooth skin, and sometimes wearing fur.

Traditional Ojibwe women, to protect themselves when they meet a bear in the woods, open their dresses and show their bodies. "It is only me, my husband," they say. Tagish women call the bear "brother," knowing that the taboo against incest will keep them safe.

All of this inter-mixing of bears and humans is not the confusion of primitive and superstitious minds. It is acknowledgment that there are no "objective observers" in this world, only participants. We eat the bear,

48

and we are the bear. The bear eats us, and the bear is us. We watch the bear, in an "objective" way, and the bear still teaches us, and its spirit is part of us. The real illusion is the one that says we are somehow separate from each other.

In us, that which is Bear remains, reminding us of our relationship with nature, our emotional and spiritual side, our ability to look within ourselves and find a balance, a center, within the great circles spinning around us every second of our lives. Without the acknowledgment of our dark, wild side, the center will remain elusive. A case could be made that, *without* the Bear, our culture will continue to suffer the confusion that lies just behind our arrogance.

49

CHAPTER FIVE

THE STORY WEAVER

DRUM-BEAT, BEAT OF DRUMS,
PEBBLE-RATTLE IN THE GOURD,
CHILD FEET IN THE HOGAN.
DRUM-BEAT, BEAT OF DRUMS,
A CHILD HAS TAUGHT HER SPIDER TO WEAVE
BEAD-WORK AT MY DOOR.
A CHILD HAS TAUGHT THESE DIMMING EYES TO SEE
THREAD-WORK IN A STAR-LIT LODGE. . .

NAVAHO LULLABY

There are about eighty thousand species of spiders worldwide. Half have not yet been seen by humans. In temperate climates such as ours, there are over two million spiders on an acre of land, 75 million on every square mile and perhaps 100 quadrillion living on planet earth. Considering that spiders feast heavily on insects, various reputable scientists have speculated about the effects of eliminating spiders from the planet. Computer projections say that if spiders were suddenly gone, ecological systems would be so severely disrupted that life as we know it would cease to exist in two to eight days.

Even without scientific techniques and computer hardware, Native Americans had a profound and deep appreciation of the Many-Leggeds. They watched the intricacies of the food web every day of their lives. It was easy to develop a sense of personal humility in the face of the billions of dramas unfolding around them. Their personal involvement in the web of life made it easy for them to see themselves as a participant in that web—a single strand in the warp and weave of the planet.

The idea for woven fabric was probably borrowed from the spider eons ago. Snares were a spider invention. With long gossamer threads held by the wind, young dispersing spiders were the world's first skydivers. The "itsy bitsy spider" has taught most of us the value of perseverance, plugging away at crawling up the water spout time after time. Our complete dependence on the seemingly insignificant, like the spider, was easy to see for Native people, because they actually looked.

When they looked carefully at spiders, they saw a creature far older than the human race. They saw a spinner and weaver, one who could create something from almost nothing. They saw spiders descending from the trees and smokeholes in long filaments. Ahh, said the Hopi, it must have been Grandmother Spider who descended into the Earth to the First World, guiding us out to our present homes. Ahh, said the Navaho, it must have been Grandmother Spider who descended from Spider Rock (in Canyon du Chelly) to create us here.

The Hopis have a metaphor for creation that serves well as a summary of evolution. In the beginning there was only space and Tawa, the Sun. The Sun, with the help of some water and lightning, created a world deep in the earth. There, insects and other tiny creatures scurried and ate each other. Tawa was unsatisfied with the First World, because none of the creatures understood beauty very well. He sent Grandmother Spider down on a long filament to change these creatures. Grandmother led them on a long journey to a cave above the First World, and on the way changed some of them into bears and coyotes and deer—the furred ones. They were closer to what the Sun had

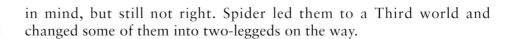

in mind, but still not right. Spider led them to a Third world and changed some of them into two-leggeds on the way.

The Third World was better, but dark and cold. Hummingbird had to bring them a fire drill from above, and with fire, they learned how to bake pots, cook meat and warm corn seeds so they would grow. But without light, the sorcerers stole virtue from the people and society degenerated. Tawa was not pleased with this world either, and sent Grandmother Spider once again, with the message that those who wanted to keep virtue should leave this place. The Elders held a council, and made a messenger from the smoke of the Pipe and some clay. It was a Swallow. They asked their messenger to fly up and investigate the footsteps they had heard above them. Swallow returned with news of an opening in the sky. The elders made a dove, a hawk, and a catbird, each of whom came back with more information. The dove saw an empty land, the hawk found mesas and trees farther away, and the catbird talked to the Owner of Fire and Death, the only being living there.

The people decided to go. Grandmother Spider, with the help of her twin grandsons and Chipmunk, the planter, sent up a sunflower, a spruce, a pine, and finally a bamboo shoot, which reached the sipapu, the opening. The people climbed out and inhabited the Fourth World, the one we know. One sorcerer sneaked out with them, so there was good and evil and death in this world. The Sun was satisfied with this world and came closer to watch. The sorcerers hide from the living light of Tawa to this day.

In honor of the four sacred directions, there are often four tries before a successful accomplishment. This statement about perseverance could have easily come from the persistence of the spider, who weaves a wind-destroyed web over and over again in the same spot. A person must ask for some knowledge four times before they will be taken seriously. A virtuous person can not deceive someone four times in a row, only three. The fourth time, they are obligated to tell the truth.

Grandmother Spider named all the people and their clans as they emerged from the sipapu. She named them Ute and Navaho and Comanche and all the others, so they could live well on the different lands she sent them to. But she also warned them never to forget that they all emerged from the same place, the same womb, the great kiva. And they have the same mother, the Earth. "The sorcerers will point out your differences," she said, "in the hopes of turning you against each other. Remember the truth."

The Muskogee people realized that the special skills of Grandmother Spider, along with the character of other animals, helped the world be what it is today. According to them, when the Earth was first created there was no light. The animals found it hard to live that way, and decided to steal the Sun from the other side of the Earth. Fox was the first to try. He grabbed the hot Sun in his mouth, it burned him and he dropped it. His mouth is still black today because of the burns. Possum tried too, with his tail, and burned all of the hair from it. Grandmother Spider tried, but she used her silk, and spun a ball around the Sun. She carried it to where the animals lived.

It was hard for everyone to crowd around the Sun as it lay on the ground, and Grandmother Spider suggested that someone put it high in the sky. No one could reach high enough, so Grandmother decided to ask the birds for help. Vulture was the only volunteer, because he could fly higher than everyone else. He put the Sun on his head and circled up, higher and higher, until he could drop the Sun where it lives today. Of course, the Sun burned all the feathers off his head and turned it red. Vulture still circles the Sun today, higher than anyone else, and the Sun's rays sometimes fan out like Grandmother Spider's web, to honor the work she did for all the plants and animals.

The spirit of cooperation, and the essential status of all creatures, was (and is) apparent to traditional Native Americans. Constant participation in the design and order of the universe is taken for granted. There is no need to dissect and separate things in the world to understand the basic truth of the design. Grandmother Spider is an Elder, an old one as elders go. That she would be a keeper of wisdom and harmony, secure in the webs she weaves, is not questioned. And she is persistent and consistent, seeing that living in harmony is a daily duty.

The Lakota people of the Northern Plains have a Spider person who is very different than the benevolent Grandmother of the Southwest. Iktome the Spider is Coyote, Raven, and the Great Hare incarnated. Iktome is good-natured, conceited, cunning, innocent and stupid. Always, this Spider is a warning against those who call themselves friends rather than showing their friendship through action.

In the Distant Time, Iktome came upon some ducks splashing in the water, having a good time. The ducks were curious about what was in her sack of silk. "Oh, just some old songs," said Iktome. The ducks pleaded with her to sing some of the old songs, and she smiled and agreed. "We will sing in the stick lodge I will build."

Iktome built a teepee of sticks, herded the ducks inside and began to sing them a song about closing their eyes and not peeking. "If you look, your eyes will turn red," said the song. The ducks were mesmerized by the song and closed their eyes tightly. The song went on and on. Finally, one of the ducks opened an eye and saw Iktome outside the teepee next to a large pile of ducks, all with their necks wrung. The duck quacked loudly and all the living ducks flew away. Most ducks now have red eyes.

Iktome wanted to have a feast, but had no pot for the ducks. She screamed loudly for someone to bring a kettle, and finally Fox showed up with one. Iktome told Fox thanks and good-bye, without asking Fox to share in the feast. As Iktome was cooking, she took a nap. Two foxes came back while Iktome slept and took turns eating and stroking Iktome's face with their tails, to keep her asleep. They put all the bare bones back in the pot. When Iktome woke up, she thought that she had cooked the ducks too long.

The message here is about paybacks: "What goes around comes around." Native people saw a natural balance in the world—what is given will always come back, and what is taken will always go away again. Given those choices, it really is better to give than receive. Again, this version of the Golden Rule was to be lived, not stated.

Iktome once had a similar experience with Muskrat. Iktome did not invite Muskrat to share her kettle of fish, which was boiling on the fire. This was against the custom of all the Plains people. Muskrat just stood there for a long time until Iktome said that the winner of a race around the pond should have all the fish. Muskrat was hesitant because he was very slow, so Iktome agreed to carry a large stone on her back. Iktome let Muskrat get ahead until Iktome could not see the sedges move as Muskrat ran through them. Iktome dropped the stone and raced around the pond, grinning. When she reached the finish, the pot was gone and the ashes were cold. Muskrat knew Iktome would not keep her word because of her refusal to share, and won the race by swimming instead of running.

Dishonesty has the effect of canceling all the rules, and one breach of honor will cause everyone to understand that there is no trust with this person.

Spider had an encounter with Coyote once, according to the Southern Ute people. Coyote found a Spider on a tree and bragged to Spider that he planned to eat it. Spider whispered to Coyote that some humans were planning to kill him, and Spider volunteered to spy on them and find what plans they had. Coyote agreed, but told Spider to hurry back. Spider didn't come back at all.

Later, Coyote ran into Spider again, sitting on another tree. Coyote once again announced that he was going to eat Spider. Spider whispered to Coyote that this tree was Chief Tree of the whole world, and if he touched the tree and closed his eyes, he would see everything in the whole world. "Just try," Spider said. Coyote tried, and Spider sneaked away. . .

A Salish story about Spider explains his appearance. Spider was a handsome young animal and a good hunter, but also a bit too proud of himself. Many of the young women liked him, but he had a test none of them could pass. He built a smoky fire when they visited, and closed the door. If they could stay inside longer than he could, he would marry them. None could.

The daughter of Beaver heard of the test and asked her father for some medicine to help. He gave her some special grease for her nose and eyes. She went to visit Spider and he built his customary fire. It was so thick inside that he couldn't see a thing. He kept talking to the young woman but she did not answer. He was worried that he had killed her with the smoke, so he ran around to the other side of the fire to find her. She burst out laughing, and he was angry at being beaten at his own test. He kicked her with all of his legs, but her father's medicine was strong—she pulled on his legs and they stretched out. Today, Spider has long legs.

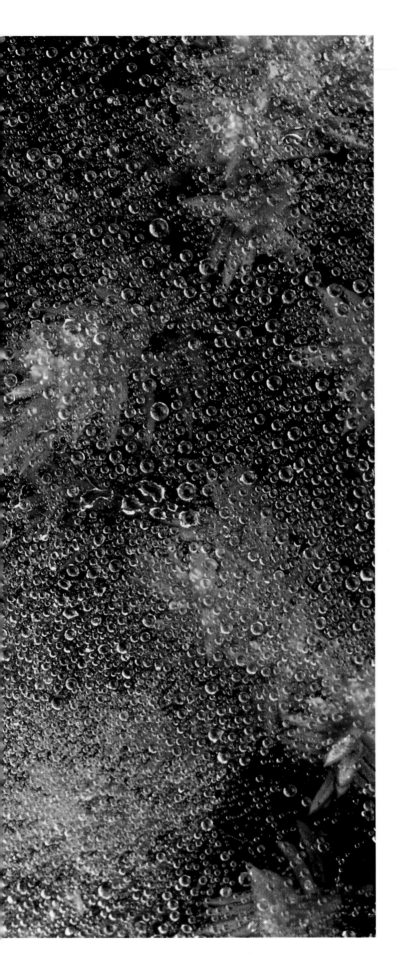

Beaver's daughter married him—he was still a good provider.

The medicine we each carry inside of us comes partly from our heritage. The wisdom of older family members is often lost in our world. We worship youth, and the net result is an irretrievable loss of the wisdom gained through experience. Our Grandmothers and Grandfathers come in all shapes, some with two legs and some with eight.

Children are not born with the phobias they are exposed to in later life. "Itsy Bitsy Spider" and "Charlotte's Web" put the real danger from spiders in its proper perspective. An Ojibwe custom has that same calming effect on very young children. When a child is born, the family that shows the proper respect for Grandmother Spider (such as not shrieking and killing her) will wake up one morning to a special gift. The Grandmother weaves a web above the child's head, leaving a small hole in the center of the web. When dreams are moving about at night, looking for sleeping humans to speak to, they must pass through the dream net woven by Grandmother Spider. The dreams with crooked paths (nightmares) are caught in the web and captured. Dreams with straight paths pass cleanly through the hole in the center, and into the child's mind.

Ojibwe women weave a net in a willow hoop, just like Grandmother Spider's, and hang it over the crib of their babies. It's a reminder of the gift of a Grandmother, and a reminder that most gifts come from places where we least expect them.

59

CHAPTER SIX

WISDOM WARRIOR

A WOLF I CONSIDERED MYSELF
BUT
I HAVE EATEN NOTHING
AND
FROM STANDING I AM TIRED OUT.

A WOLF I CONSIDERED MYSELF
BUT
THE OWLS ARE HOOTING
AND
THE NIGHT I FEAR.

TETON LAKOTA SONG

Native Americans often used the wolf as an ideal, often to point out their own limitations, such as fear of the dark. The Blackfoot/Blood/Piegans of the northern Rockies spoke of a harmonious life as "traveling the wolf trail." Many traditional people thought that the eyes of the wolf and the eyes of the human were the same eyes. On almost all continents, our ancestors learned to hunt in packs effectively. Without wolves as teachers and mentors of the hunt, we probably would not be here.

Wolves taught us about cooperation and the value of our extended families. They taught us about protectiveness and about fidelity to our tribe. They taught us how the social system in a tribe functions smoothly, and with the best interests of everyone in mind. We watched them, and learned how to "howl at the moon" in celebration. They showed us how to move through the world carefully and quietly.

It has been said that wolves are the creatures most like us, but I think we have the seniority system mixed up. We are the creatures most patterned after wolves.

Native Americans rarely looked at the wolf as a competitor or enemy. If game was scarce, the wolves would be gone. The presence of wolves was a good sign. The good hunter watched wolves for signs of bison or elk in the air, and he never killed without offering some meat to his assistant and scout. Eventually, this relationship blossomed into one in which we call the wolf "man's best friend." Long ago, the wolves and humans realized their brotherhood, and made a truce. The wolves still observe it.

We westerners have killed about two million wolves since we moved to North America. Wolves have killed none, *none*, of us. For ten thousand years, Native people observed the truce. The Blackfoot and Lakota believe that a gun used to shoot a wolf will never shoot straight again. It would be a curse on the brotherly relationship akin to the story of Cain and Abel.

A Blackfoot woman named Sits By The Door was captured in a Crow raid and carried hundreds of miles to Crow country as a prisoner. She escaped with the help of a Crow woman, but nearly starved when she was still far from her people. She watched helplessly as a wolf came close by and lay down, probably waiting for her to die. She told her story to the wolf. Next morning there was a freshly killed buffalo calf next to her on the ground. She ate, regained some of her strength, and resumed her journey. She still could barely walk, so the wolf walked next to her and supported part of her weight. They traveled together for days, and the wolf continued to bring kills to her. By the time she reached her people, she was as strong as before she left. She camped just outside the village because the wolf was still wild, but the camp dogs eventually ran it away. The woman became sick and eventually

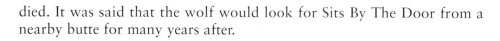

died. It was said that the wolf would look for Sits By The Door from a nearby butte for many years after.

The relationship between wolves and humans is summarized well by the story of Sits By The Door. The camp dogs were not comfortable with their wolf origins, nor are people today comfortable with theirs. Perhaps our wild sides do still wait for us, just outside of the camp. . .

A Lakota story is very similar. A woman was hurt and left behind by her people. She ran out of food and nearly starved, but came upon a wolf den and crawled inside. At first the members of the pack were suspicious and afraid of her, but they still brought food to the pups, which she shared. Eventually, she was strong enough to snare rabbits and help with the hunting. She stayed with the pack for many years. One day the oldest wolf smelled humans coming, and strangely, the woman did also. They were her own people, and she realized she must return to them. She reunited herself with her village very slowly because their smell was so strong it made her sick. But she brought with her the skills of the wolf. She knew from the wolf talk she heard at night, and from her sensitive nose, how to predict weather far in advance and to alert the village when game or other humans were nearby.

This story shows how Native Americans saw the process of education. Learning the ways of the wolves took sacrifice, risk, hardship and many years for the wolf-woman. For them, learning is never accomplished by creating a completely artificial situation (we call it school) for the student. Education is done by placing a willing student in the presence of an elder, and then living life as it comes. Learning is *only* about life—it is not done for its own sake.

Humans fear what they don't understand. Red Riding Hood, Three Little Pigs, Peter and the Wolf, crying wolf, wolfing food, wolf at the door, thrown to the wolves, werewolves—these are examples of the wolf legacy from Europe and America. A Pawnee story tells that it was once that way with the Native American nations too.

Creator, with the assistance of lightning and thunder, sang, shook rattles, and struck the ground and water with their clubs. In this way they created everything we see today—except one. They forgot about the Wolf. A great red star in the southeast sky was curious about creation and changed itself to a form that could run across the land and see things far and wide. This form was Wolf.

Thunder picked hundreds of stars from the sky, put them in a whirlwind sack and went down to examine the creation for himself. Thunder explored many places, occasionally putting the sack down and watching with amusement as the stars would spill out and try to run away, on two legs. He sucked them back in the whirlwind sack and explored new places.

Wolf had picked up Thunder's trail and followed until he found Thunder asleep. Thinking there may be food in the bag, Wolf quietly nipped at the strings of the whirlwind, and out poured two-leggeds, who ran off and set up camps all over creation. An old woman from the bag adopted Wolf and fed him buffalo meat. One day hunters came back from a hunt empty-handed and angry. They wanted to blame someone. When they turned around to look behind them, they saw Thunder roaring their way, himself angry at losing his two-legged toys. They were afraid, and in their fear and anger, the hunters shot Wolf and killed him.

Thunder was angry that the two-leggeds had run away, but he was even more angry that they had killed something just because they didn't understand it. Thunder roared at them for being afraid of mystery, and told them that they were no longer welcome in the whirlwind sack, where they would have lived forever. He told them that mystery would always be replaced with another mystery, and the new one was the mystery of death. Since that time, the Earth has lived with death nearby.

Today, the Pawnee call themselves the Skidi Pawnee, the Wolf People. Their scouts are legendary, operating just like a wolf pack in hunting and warfare. The metaphor of this story is remarkably similar to our world. We kill what we don't understand, and it will, with certainty, bring more death into our world. The recent re-introduction of wolves into my home area in the west has humans seeing them as a scapegoat yet again. Contrary to thousands of years of hard evidence, the newly-arrived wolves are seen as demons who will destroy, indiscriminately, all the work that humans have done to make the world safe for cattle. Perhaps the concept of indiscriminate destruction is too close to home for humans. We tend to see in others what is buried far inside of our own hearts. Wolves will come and go, as they always have, but the sense of emptiness in our own lives will not be removed by the removal of the wolf. Nothing very important changes quickly in this world. We re-live moral crises over and over again, resisting lessons from our elders, and killing the creation which makes and sustains us.

"What good are they?" is a question which reveals most about the person asking the question. Wolves teach us about mystery—they are not under our illusion of control. They once taught us how to hunt in packs and survive. They only live on land which is not yet ravaged by greed. They remind us that we are not the center of the universe, that dominion is an illusion. By comparison, what good are we?

On the medicine wheel, the North, Wolf, represents intelligence, knowledge and wisdom. The intelligence and knowledge parts are easy for humans, but wisdom comes from a balance of experience and self-knowledge. Cleverness is no substitute for having a direction in life or being comfortable with the path we choose. The Wolf Trail is not as worn these days. Tracks of two-leggeds wander aimlessly. We are usually looking for someone else to follow, while the trail of wisdom grows over.

In a Seneca myth, Wolf and Raccoon are having an argument. Raccoon was hurling insults at Wolf from the safety of a tree. Wolf was howling at Raccoon about his insulting behavior. Wolf soon realized that he would not change Raccoon. Raccoon had to change himself. Wolf was bored and went to sleep. Raccoon sneaked out of the tree and pasted pitch on Wolf's sleeping eyes. Wolf woke up and could not see, so he called to his friends the birds to help him. The birds liked Wolf because he always left a small part of his kills for them. They pecked at the pitch until it cracked and broke loose. Wolf was grateful and asked if there was anything he could do for them. The birds were all the same kind, and had always wanted to be painted, so Wolf painted them many beautiful colors, all different.

The imagination of wolf is hinted at in this story, if we consider the thousands of colors representing thousands of species of birds. It also is a not-so-subtle reminder to keep good relationships with others because it is *right*, not just because you will get something from them. Wolf could not have foretold that he would someday need the help of some dull little birds, but he treated them with respect anyway. As it turns out, it was the wise thing to do.

The Kutenai people know why the wolves and deer are at war to this day. Wolf was once married to Doe, but she was from another tribe and made moccasins to fit a hoof. Every time Wolf would wear the moccasins, they hurt his feet, and they would punch deep into the snow when he tried to run. Wolf realized that this relationship was not exactly made in heaven and told Doe to go back to her own people.

Wolf moved in with his own family. One day they went on a raid and discovered the Deer village. His relatives killed all the deer except Buck, who barely escaped. Buck ran to the home of Fish, where he asked for Fish's help. Fish agreed to help, but warned Buck that he must remain motionless for the trick to work.

Wolf tracked Buck to the river home of Fish, and cleared his throat to announce his presence. Buck stood still behind a robe in the lodge, and Wolf came in to talk to ask Fish if he had seen Buck. Fish lied, and said he had heard sounds on the other side of the river. Wolf went outside to look, and Fish put grass on his fire, making smoke which went out the smoke hole and shaped itself into a deer. Wolf chased it, and Buck went the opposite direction.

Fish called to Wolf on the other side, reminding him that Buck was his brother-in-law, and that he should not kill everyone in the Deer village. Wolf was ashamed at his greedy warfare, and agreed not to kill all the deer. To this day, deer often escape by standing motionless, and wolves leave some deer behind, to have young. The new deer replace the ones killed and eaten in the raids.

To Native people, ecology was not something taught from a book. It was "the way things are," to be lived on a daily basis. It did not take much observation of "the way things are" to realize that the deer and wolf are dependent on each other, and that the elimination of deer would be a very stupid thing for the wolf to do, even though he easily could. The agreement between the wolves and deer is that the wolf will pursue only hard enough to catch *some* deer, but not all. It took our culture until the 1950s to discover this basic principle of predator-prey relationships. All we had to do was ask. . .

Even though Wolf was Coyote's older brother, say the Northern Paiute, they were very different from each other. Wolf studied and learned the habits of many animals. This knowledge allowed Wolf to become a great hunter. Coyote was lazier, and fed from the kills Wolf made. But Coyote was always jealous of another animal's skills, so he asked Wolf to teach him how to hunt. Wolf took Coyote out to the mountains. He looked at a pile of brush and said, "Certain rabbits, come out to me." A few rabbits came out and wolf killed them. Coyote couldn't wait to try this method his own way. Next day, he found a pile of brush and said, "All you rabbits, come out to me." Coyote killed all the rabbits and ate them, laughing. He went to another pile and said the same words, but nothing happened. Coyote shrugged and found some holes. He called out all the groundhogs and ate them, but the next bunch of holes had no groundhogs.

Coyote returned home and Wolf could tell from Coyote's round belly that Coyote had not hunted the right way. Still, he said nothing to his little brother. That night, Wolf had a dream that some animals were going to come and try to kill him. He asked his little brother to gather some arrow-sticks from the bottom of the mountain. He warned Coyote that he shouldn't go to the top of the mountain because that would not leave Wolf enough time to make the arrows. Coyote, of course, did go to the top, where he saw the animal war party coming. He ran back to Wolf, empty-handed, and warned Wolf about what he already knew. Still, Wolf said nothing.

When the animals came for Wolf, he shut Coyote in a mud house and told him to stay there and not peek outside. Coyote heard a great battle, which went on for hours. He couldn't stand it, and asked a mouse to dig him a hole just big enough to see the action. As soon as Coyote looked, Wolf turned to look at Coyote and was killed.

Coyote was sad, but realized that he might have an opportunity for revenge. He dressed up like a woman and made a bundle to look like

baby. He lured the animal women away from their village, tied their hair together and had his way with them. Then he remembered his brother. He went to the home of the Chief and stole the head of Wolf. Coyote cried over his brother and as he grieved every day, Wolf gradually came back to life.

The difference between Coyote and us is that he has the luxury of being able to undo his mistakes whenever he chooses. In this story, he does not listen to the wisdom of his brother, his Elder. We have the same choice in front of us. We can carefully use some of the Earth for our own benefit, or we can choose to believe that we have a right to it all. We can do our work, or doodle away our time with diversions. We can accept those things which we should not see, or peek out of the hole, never realizing that just because we *can* doesn't mean we *should*. Always, out there in the night, Wolf is watching patiently to see if any wisdom is rubbing off.

Someday perhaps we can look at Wolf the way Wolf sees us. According to Native people, we have the right eyes for the job.

CHAPTER SEVEN

Salmon
GIFT OF THE WATERS

STOP. I SEE SOMETHING.
WE COME IN RED CANOES.
THE SALMON COME!

STOP. I SEE SOMETHING.
PART OF US IS SPREADING SOFTLY OVER THE WATER.
THE SALMON BLEEDS FROM MY KILLING CLUB.

STOP. I SEE SOMETHING.
WE COME AGAIN, EVER FAITHFUL.
MY FAMILY WILL BE STRONG AGAIN.

KOYUKON RIDDLE SONG

For thousands of years on the Northwest coast of North America, the return of the salmon was a miracle beyond comprehension. There are narrows on my home river, the Salmon, where the red backs of salmon were solid from shore to shore only forty years ago. Natives on the Northwest Coast developed an intricate ceremonial and artistic community, mostly because they had an abundance of leisure time. Food-gathering was not a time-consuming process. The salmon came almost every year, and they came by the millions.

Inland, the spring and fall runs of salmon were anticipated and celebrated, but never taken for granted. Occasional weather- or disease-related interruptions of the run caused great hardship. People hoped that their relationship with the salmon was healthy and respectful enough to ensure their return. If the run was lower than usual, Native people looked to their own behavior as one of the root causes. In the Native view, any breach of contract with the natural world had immediate and far-reaching consequences. The awareness of interdependence was so strong, people felt their thoughts and attitudes must remain pure. The connections between themselves and the rest of nature were physical, emotional, spiritual and psychic. The boundaries around them were much less important than the connections. They were as much a part of the salmon as they were an individual.

It is no small problem to the communication between Western society and Native Americans that the dominant culture subscribes to the concept of rugged individualism. We see all humans (and other species, for that matter) as islands unto themselves. This way of thinking is completely interwoven with our social, economic, political and even spiritual institutions. Considering the effects of this individualistic world view on the health of our planet, we have to wonder which perspective is more "accurate." The Western world view is more *scientifically* accurate, to be sure, but science is a *product* of the Western world view. Science, for all its professed objectivity, is very culturally biased when it examines the kind of "reality" traditional Native Americans perceive. When a Tlingit operates under a moral code, which includes "not offending the salmon," it is just as rational to their world as insurance policies are to us. Scientific cause and effect operates only in the physical world, to the exclusion of other possibilities. Natives take a broader view.

Only in affluent cultures can food be taken for granted. The kind of affluence we experience in North America is a very recent (and rare) historical occurrence. Inside layers of cellophane and styrofoam is a fillet of salmon which has chosen to take pity on us and give itself away. But we rarely see it that way.

The Tlingit do see it that way. Once, not terribly long ago, a Tlingit boy who wore a copper necklace grabbed a piece of dried salmon to chew on.

The salmon had some surface mold on it, but was fine to eat if the mold was scraped off. Because he was young, the boy had never seen a time when salmon meat was scarce. He threw the salmon on the ground with some disgust. His mother warned him that the salmon did not like being treated this way, but he ignored her, stalked outside and went to the rocks by the sea.

He tied a hook and some meat to a string and threw it in the sea—he was trying to catch a gull to eat. A huge gull flew around the rocks and grabbed the bait. Before the boy could react, he was pulled off the rocks and into the water. As he descended into the ocean, he saw a canoe coming toward him, under the water. Inside were people who wore shiny silver clothing. They invited him into their canoe and paddled to their village. They adopted this boy with the copper necklace and called him "Half-Moldy Boy."

Later, the boy was hungry. The Silver People told him to go to the next village and eat one of the people there. They warned him to burn all of the bones when he was done eating. "If you do this, you will be surprised when you come back here," they told him. He went to the village and killed a person, who turned into a fish as he died. Half-Moldy Boy ate the fish, but was so anxious to see the surprise, he threw the bones into the fire and left. When he arrived at his own village, he saw the surprise. It was the man he had killed, still alive. The man was walking around moaning and holding his back. Half-Moldy Boy realized he had not done his part correctly, and he ran back to the other village and looked at his fire. Sure enough, there was still one back bone which had not burned, so he built another fire and burned it. When he returned to his village again, the man was fine.

Life became routine for a while and Half-Moldy Boy learned the ways, the songs and the prayers of the Silver People. One day, the whole village stepped into their canoes and paddled to the rivers. They all knew which river they were to paddle, and the boy found the canoe which was going up the river he knew. There were places, waterfalls, where the Silver People had to leap high out of the canoe in order to keep going. Half-Moldy Boy leaped out at the fourth waterfall and saw his old village on the shore. Before he fell back into the water he was caught in a net. The woman who caught him looked in disbelief at this Salmon with a copper necklace around its gills. "This is my Son!" she said.

His mother took him home and asked the advice of a Shaman—she missed her son and wanted him back. He gave her some salmon oil, and every morning she put a drop on the salmon with the copper necklace, and then covered it with a blanket. For four days she did this, and on the fourth morning she pulled back her blanket and her son was there, sleeping. His name was Salmon Boy after that, and he grew up to teach the Tlingit the ways, the songs and the prayers of the Salmon People.

The Tlingit saw the Salmon People as forgiving and benevolent—they returned to give themselves away almost every year despite the transgressions of the humans. But to waste, or take the Salmon for granted, was beyond forgivable. It demanded re-education. In order to see the world clearly, all Tlingit need to see themselves clearly—they are made of the Salmon, which they eat all year as their main diet. The physical interchange of atoms and molecules is easy to understand from a scientific perspective, but the Tlingit took the interchange as a figurative (spiritual) process as well as a literal one. They and the Salmon are one, *any* way we look at it. To waste Salmon is to abuse themselves. "Do unto others" was not a rule reserved only for the treatment of other humans. "People" come in all shapes, sizes and colors, even silver. . .

The continual return of the salmon is a mystery to science, but we have learned some things about them and other anadromous (ocean fish, returning to rivers to spawn) species, such as the steelhead trout. Salmon and steelhead return upriver thousands of miles and spawn in exactly the same spot where they hatched years ago. They find their way by tasting the unique mix of water chemicals of their home stream. The ability to taste their way home from that distance and through that many obstacles is beyond human comprehension. Science can *name* and *describe* the process, but understanding it is another story.

Although Native people in salmon country had only observation skills, with no special radio-tagging and gas chromatography equipment at their disposal, they still understood, somehow, that Salmon return to their home spawning beds. Perhaps they remember their own trips, when they were Salmon. Perhaps they realize that all species wish to return home when they are mature, to revisit their past, and be caught up and eaten by the culture that spawned them. Perhaps they make no distinction between either of those possibilities. . .

The lesson is relatively clear. When we see the *similarities* between us and others, instead of being scientifically obsessed with the differences, it opens a whole world of possibilities. We can see ourselves in the other person or the other species, and appreciate that we are not nearly as alone and isolated as we sometimes think. We have relatives everywhere we look.

So where did the miracle of Salmon come from? In another Tlingit tale, Raven married the daughter of Fog-Over-The-Water. He gets hungry and asks his wife for some food. She washes her hands over a basket and a salmon appears in the basket. Every time Raven gets hungry, she does the same. She produces many salmon and they dry them for future use. Later, Raven and his wife have a quarrel and he throws a piece of salmon at her and hits her. She runs out of the lodge and Raven pursues her out the door, but when he grabs for her, she is fog, and his hands pass through her body. Raven realizes he had a good thing and tries to convince Fog-Over-The-Water to find his daughter and send her back. The father refuses. Raven has not treated her with the respect she deserves.

The idea of Salmon coming from the fog shows the feeling of mystery surrounding the origin of the staple creature in Tlingit economics. The fog often shrouds visual reality on the Northwest Coast. Since the fog is an almost daily occurrence (washing its hands and making salmon), it would be logical to make a connection to the sheer numbers of fish that run the rivers each year. The Tlingit were, and are, comfortable with the mystery.

In a Kwakiutl story, Raven robs a grave where twins are buried. (When twins are born, one of the twins represents the alter-ego of the other—in this case the alter-ego of humans is the salmon.) One of the spirit twins admits to Raven that she used to be a salmon. Raven uses his powers to wash the woman and revive her. Then she creates salmon for him in ways similar to the Tlingit story. When she puts her little finger in the water, the salmon turn and swim upstream. When she washes her hands, salmon appear. When she swims, the rivers are full of salmon. Raven goes off to do his Raven business, and she feeds other animals while he is gone. Raven returns and sees salmon pieces stuck in the teeth of the other animals. Raven is angry and drives her out, with the same result as the Tlingit version.

The Bella Coola, Haida, Oweekeno, Chilcotin and Shuswap versions have Raven kidnapping the daughter of the Salmon Chief. Raven is invited to partake in a feast after the Salmon Chief's four daughters swim out and each catch a salmon. Raven likes the salmon and holds a bone in his mouth so he can later create salmon from it. One of the daughter's noses starts to bleed, and the Chief realizes what Raven is up to. Raven abducts one of the daughters and escapes in a canoe. The sisters put holes in the other canoes because the kidnapped daughter likes Raven anyway, and they help her out.

In a Kwakiutl version, the sisters turn into salmon and Raven pretends the bone is a blanket pin. One of the daughters is therefore missing a collarbone. Later, in all the versions, Raven always manages to insult the salmon and then loses his wife.

The story leading up to this one in Bella Coola culture has Raven unsuccessfully carving salmon out of wood, then realizing he needs a bone from the real salmon to build them. A Tahltan story often told after the main creation tale is one about Raven stealing salmon eggs and putting them far upstream, which forces the salmon to migrate there every year.

Following the creation of salmon, Raven must use his blundering trickery to catch salmon. Most of the northwest Natives have a story about Raven digging four holes in the river and daring the salmon to jump in the air at the waterfall and knock Raven over. On the fourth try, Raven succeeds. He then enlists the Crows to get some kettles for cooking. They bring only seashells time after time, so Raven gets disgusted and goes himself. The Crows steal and eat the fish. Raven gets even by throwing ashes on the Crows, turning them black. However, Raven turns himself black in the process.

In a Salishan story, Salmon wins a beautiful wife by raiding the Kalispels. They live in a lodge above a gigantic falls. Rattlesnake becomes jealous and plots to kill Salmon. He makes special arrows and shoots Salmon in the head. Salmon falls in the river and floats downstream. Salmon's wife is distraught and howls in grief. Three wolves hear her and take the woman to cook and sew for them.

Meanwhile, Salmon's body floats to the mouth of the river and washes up on a sand bar. There it stays for many months until only a pile of bones remains. Mouse, who is, as usual, exploring, discovers Salmon's bones and is sad. (Mouse likes Salmon.) He and his wife live in the pile of bones and smear oil on the bones every day, eventually restoring Salmon to life.

Salmon swims upstream to the falls and finds Rattlesnake there in his lodge. After he sees Salmon coming, Rattlesnake pretends to sing a mourning song for him. Salmon pretends to not remember what the snake had done to him, and when he is close, sets Rattlesnake's lodge on fire and burns him alive. Then Salmon discovers that his wife has been taken by the wolves. He kills two of them, but decides to let the third wolf live if it agrees to stay far back in the timber. Salmon takes his wife to a new lodge in the water below the falls. He will never venture above the giant falls again.

Most Native American stories that deal with the results of disrespect have turned out to be prophetic. Between my house in Idaho and the Pacific Ocean, there are eleven "giant waterfalls" in the form of dams. The water from the reservoirs irrigates desert land and provides power for the aluminum industry. Fish ladders have been built around the dams, but the upstream migration of salmon has proven to be only a small part of the problem. The young salmon fry, it turns out, get lost in the still water of the reservoirs. And a high percentage of the ones who find their way to the dam get sucked into the knife-blades of the turbines. If salmon can't make it to the sea, they certainly won't return home someday. It is ironic that, in our quest for a higher quality of life, we often lower another part of that quality somewhere else. In the name of getting rich, we get poorer all the time. We are, whether we like to admit it or not, "Half-Moldy Boy," throwing down the salmon, pretending that we don't need it. This is not the first time our culture has thumbed its nose at a miracle.

CHAPTER EIGHT

THE MESSENGER

STRIKE YOU OUR LAND
WITH CURVED HORNS.
BENDING OUR BODIES,
BREATHE FIRE UPON US.
NOW WITH FEET
TRAMPLING THE EARTH,
LET YOUR HOOVES
THUNDER OVER US.

OJIBWE BUFFALO DANCE

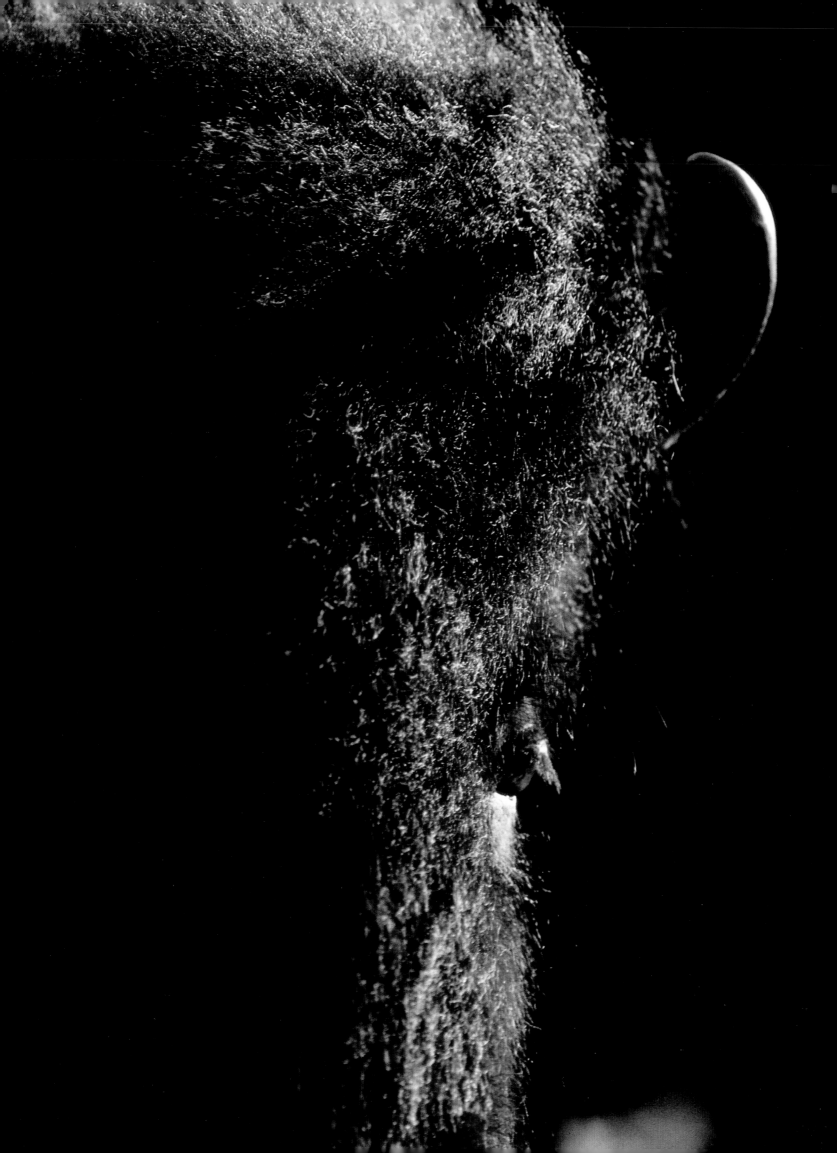

No animal is more associated with Native America than the buffalo. The plains, mountain valleys and even open pockets of land in the eastern woods held vast herds of these huge shaggy creatures. As with the salmon on the northwest coast, buffalo were synonymous with life to the Plains people. Offending the Buffalo Spirit, taking any chance that the herds might not come, was suicidal. Most prairie Natives were nomadic, allowing them to follow the bison, or anticipate where the great herds might be later. The teepee, the travois, and even the widespread use of the horse—these all came into the service of Native Americans because of the buffalo.

Nothing on the prairie was more powerful than the buffalo, physically or spiritually. The bulls weighed nearly a ton and could turn so fast that most animals could not out-maneuver a charge. Buffalo-fighting, with matadors and toreadors, would be a severe natural selection pressure on humans stupid enough to try it. Today, in our national parks, bison kill far more human photographers and campers than do grizzlies. They are a large, unpredictable and dangerous animal. The Plains Native Americans, Cheyenne, Lakota, Crow, Pawnee, Arapaho, Assiniboine, Kiowa, Plains Cree, Omaha, Comanche, Kansa, and Shoshone, had cultures completely interwoven with the buffalo. And, when they hunted them from horseback with bows and arrows, many hunters paid the ultimate price.

On the medicine wheel, the buffalo represented the north direction, the place of wisdom, renewal and personal power based on knowledge. The color of the north is white, the color of winter snows. When the color and the buffalo mixed together, the result (a rare white buffalo) was a powerful and compelling message to the people. The Lakota trace the spiritual origins of their culture to the visit of one such omen.

Long ago, before they had horses, two Lakota scouts were sent out to look for the herds. Their people were starving. They searched for many days, but saw nothing to hunt. One day they looked west from the top of a hill and saw a woman walking toward them. She had a very eerie quality about her. She was dressed in a buffalo robe, but it was pure white. One scout recognized her as a very good and powerful being and he felt all the positive emotions inside of him well up. The other scout was afraid, angry, jealous, and lusted after this woman because he had not seen a woman for a long time. He reached for her and was struck by a lightning bolt, leaving a pile of bones.

White Buffalo Calf Woman told the other scout she wished to bring a medicine bundle to his people. It was a gift from the Buffalo People. She told him to build a medicine lodge in his village, and that she would be there after four days. He did as he was told.

When she came to the village, the people welcomed her and gave her the seat of honor in the lodge circle. She gave them some sage to smudge the lodge and clear the minds of the people. Inside the bundle she carried a pipe bowl made of red stone and a stem made of wood. She explained that the red bowl represented the blood of the Animal People, including them, and the stem characterized all things green and growing. The smoke from the kinnikinnik (bearberry leaves and dogwood bark) represented the wind spirit which moves through all things, and binds them together. She showed them how to fill the pipe, offering kinnikinnik to the four directions, the Earth Mother and the Sky Father. This should be done "sunwise," starting with the east (birth), then to the south (growth), the west (elder years) and to the north (death and renewal). They should hold and pass the pipe in the same direction around the circle, swinging the stem around the bowl in the same direction. In this way the people would always remember the circles of life, death, rain, migration, seasons, days, moons and moods.

"The Pipe should always be smoked in silence," she said, "so you can remember what I have said today." She stood up, went outside, and rolled on the ground. She stood up again as a yellow buffalo. She rolled three more times, standing as a green buffalo, a black buffalo and finally as a white buffalo. She walked away over the horizon. As long as the people remembered, the buffalo remained around their camps and gave themselves away when the people needed them.

In recent months, a white buffalo calf was born on a buffalo farm in the Midwest. It has been visited by thousands of people, who are waiting for a new message from an old, old Messenger. The great herds have been gone for a hundred years now. The new people on this continent did not hear the message. Perhaps the buffalo will give us another chance.

Buffalo skulls have symbolized the message power of the buffalo. Shamans used them as intermediaries, recalling the time when we all spoke a language that everyone could understand. That language is based on silence. Traditional Native people still feel that silence is greater than speech, in honor of the animals, trees and rocks who move quietly through life. The first step in re-learning any language is to listen, in respectful silence. When a story is told in Native company, no one asks a question, offers a comment or whispers to someone else. In order to listen hard, the people receiving the gift of the story don't even look at the storyteller—eye contact is a potential distraction, and is seen as disrespectful of the Elder who speaks.

Coyote, who has considerable power and not much humility, still feared the power of the buffalo. The Salish of central and northern Washington blame Coyote for the lack of buffalo on their side of the Rocky Mountains. The story they tell has very similar variations among the Kutenai and Kalispel people.

Coyote found a Buffalo skull on the prairie. Remembering all the times that the Buffalo had chased him and scared him half to death, he decided to get revenge. He spat on the skull, kicked it, threw it down over and over again until he was exhausted. He started to walk away, but he heard a thundering noise behind him. He looked back and nothing was there. The noise got louder and louder until he turned to see Buffalo bearing down on him. He ran, but Buffalo gained on him. Coyote, in a panic, used his power to make some trees, and he jumped into one just as Buffalo was about to gore him. Buffalo pounded and slashed the tree until it fell, and Coyote jumped into the next one. The same thing happened three times, and finally Coyote, from the fourth and last tree, begged to have one last smoke from his pipe. Buffalo agreed. He needed a rest anyway.

Buffalo refused to smoke with Coyote, but in their conversation, Coyote learned that this old bull had been driven away from his herd by a young bull. Coyote offered to build Buffalo some new sharp horns in exchange for his life. Buffalo liked the idea. Coyote built the horns long and sharp, and Buffalo went back to his herd and beat the young bull. Buffalo offered Coyote one of his cows as a gift for his help in regaining his herd, but he admonished Coyote to never kill the cow. Instead, Coyote could have all the meat he ever needed by slicing off a small piece of the cow when he was hungry. He must use a flint knife and rub the spot with ashes—it would then immediately heal.

Coyote did this for a while, but wanted some buffalo liver to eat. Thinking that Buffalo would never know, he killed the cow and ate the liver. While he was eating, crows and magpies came from everywhere and ate the rest of the cow. Coyote decided to make soup from the bones, and just then an old woman appeared and offered to cook the soup for Coyote. He was flattered, so he took a nap while she was cooking. He dreamed about being chased, and woke up with a start. The woman was running away with the soup. He chased her for a long time, but she kept just ahead of him and taunted him as she ran. Coyote finally gave up.

He went back to the Old Buffalo and meekly asked for another cow. He was amazed to see his young cow and the old woman both there, grazing with the herd. Buffalo chased him away over the Great Mountains. Now Coyote lives in Salish Country, but Buffalo does not.

Long after this story happened, the white market hunters of the late 1800s played the role of Coyote, killing the herds by the thousands instead of taking only what they could use. The crows and magpies came by the thousands and cleaned the meat down to the bones. The Old Woman Wind came too, and she sang and moaned for years through the skeletons of millions of buffalo. The herds have never come back.

The Lakota tell of strange things that happen in the night. One of the strangest happened the night some mice decided to have a dance in the empty skull of a buffalo. They beat a tiny drum and sang in little squeaks, dancing all night in a circle around a tiny fire. The mice made a lot of commotion and woke the birds, who tweeted, and the wolves, who howled. The mice danced on and on, eventually closing their eyes and wagging their heads back and forth, almost in a trance.

Suddenly, there was a loud grunt and everything stopped. The mice opened their eyes and saw two fiery eyes looking back in at them

through the eye sockets of the skull. They scattered in all directions, and within a second or two everything was silent. No one ever knew for sure whose eyes they were. Some suspected the spirit of the Buffalo was angry, and others thought that the animals who were wakened played a trick on the rowdy mice. To this day, mice do their work silently, in the dark, and humans fill buffalo skulls with sage so no one can get inside and insult the spirit of the Buffalo.

Mouse and Buffalo had a confrontation once, much earlier in time. This Mouse was a little different than most mice. He was quite bold because he understood the power of small things, like himself. Buffalo came to this Mouse's meadow one day and began to eat. Mouse knew that the Buffalo would trim the grass so Mouse would have nowhere to hide, and he didn't like that. He challenged the Buffalo to a fight for the meadow.

Buffalo thought it was a joke, and told Mouse to be quiet or he would step on him. Mouse was defiant, and told Buffalo to try. Buffalo's eyes became red and his nostrils flared. He trampled Mouse, and when he lifted his feet, there was no squashed Mouse anywhere. Buffalo was sure that Mouse was obliterated. At that moment he heard a scratching sound and felt something gnawing inside his ear! Buffalo went wild with pain, pawed at the ground, ran in circles and stopped. He was shaking. Mouse jumped down to the ground and asked if he wanted to surrender. Buffalo was really angry this time and stomped Mouse for a long time. When he was tired of killing Mouse, he stopped to rest. He felt the gnawing in his other ear. This time, Mouse didn't stop, and Buffalo went wild with pain, and ran in circles until he dropped dead.

Mouse stood on top of the huge Buffalo and called for someone to bring him a knife—he was going to dress out the Buffalo and eat it. Fox heard the call and came running. Mouse demanded that Fox dress out the Buffalo, and agreed to give Fox some of the meat. When Fox was done, Mouse cut off a tiny piece of liver and gave it to Fox. He swallowed it quickly, and asked for another piece. Mouse called him greedy, and gave him a blood clot to eat. Fox asked for some meat for his wife, and Mouse reluctantly gave him a foot of the Buffalo, Fox asked if he could have a little more for his children, who were starving. Mouse grumbled about overpaying Fox for the work, but agreed to give him the head of the Buffalo. As soon as Mouse gave Fox the head, Fox jumped on Mouse and ate him.

Mouse lost his gift, the power of humility and discovery. He gave away what he thought was unimportant, the head of a Buffalo, because of his clouded vision. His was the first Napoleon complex. Bravery was a good quality, but Mouse became arrogant with his victory. He paid.

A story from historical times predicted the effects the New Americans would have on the buffalo when they arrived from the east. In 1845, people of the plains were beginning to see the first white traders in their land. A party of Northern Cheyenne, camped at the foot of the Medicine Bow Mountains, began to prepare for a storm that a shaman had dreamed about. It snowed three to four feet on the flats, but the weather warmed quickly and began to melt the snow. Two days later, the temperature dropped dramatically and froze a hard crust on the deep snow.

There were many buffalo in that area at the time. They could not break the crust to get to food, and as they tried to move, the crust cut their legs and tendons like thousands of knives. The prairie was littered with dark bodies and blood trails. Even the scavengers seemed terrified by the bellows of dying buffalo. The Cheyenne moved their camp as soon as they were able, and never camped there again. As they were leaving, one of the advance scouts saw a small herd of buffalo making their way into the high mountains. They were all white, like the snowy crust. Buffalo were never seen on those plains again, even though there was good grass there, and there were other herds in that region.

The Kiowa tell of the end of the buffalo, and for all purposes, the end of a Nation of people too. When the white man came, building railroads and raising cattle, the Buffalo, who had a contract with the Native People, tore up the railroad tracks and chased the cattle off the range. They loved the Red People and the People loved them. They were brothers who exchanged many gifts between each other. The whites sent the horse soldiers to kill Kiowa, and the hunters to kill Buffalo. Each hunter killed a hundred buffalo per day, the hides were piled high on the railroad cars, and the carcasses left to rot on the prairie.

The people had never seen such disrespect of the powerful Messenger. The waste was beyond the comprehension of a people who were careful to use every last sinew and bone chip when they killed. They could not imagine the amount of fear and hate needed to fuel such carnage and destruction. These could not be real humans doing this. . .

The Buffalo could no longer protect the Kiowa, and apologized for failing to do so. The Buffalo held a council and decided they must go to a place where the white humans could not go. They offered to take the Kiowa with them, but the Kiowa decided to stay on their land, the place they had been for thousands of years. The next morning, in the mist before dawn, the Buffalo People walked to the foot of a large mountain. The mountain opened up and swallowed the Buffalo forever.

When a person does not acknowledge his or her own mistakes, it is called denial. Once, ten thousand years ago, the first people on this continent

were drunk with their own technology. Their fluted spear points were a huge leap ahead— they could now throw their spears at the powerful mastodon and wooly rhinoceros from a distance instead of suicidally running up to them and stabbing. They took the mammoth, the cave bear, the giants of many kinds, from the earth forever. They spent ten thousand years learning how to do it right, doing penance. Now it is our turn.

We have taken sixty million buffalo, the passenger pigeon, the wolf, the prairie, the soil, the open spaces—and we have decimated an entire race of wise and gentle people. We call it progress, and we lecture the world about human rights.

It is clear that the Buffalo will not come back from inside the mountain until the New Americans begin to understand themselves. They need stories of their own, to carry the same important thoughts found among Native tellers. A new White Buffalo Calf is now among us. Perhaps this is a beginning.

CHAPTER NINE

Eagle
THE SACRED SEER

I AM AN EAGLE.
THE SMALL WORLD LAUGHS AT MY DEEDS,
BUT THE GREAT SKY KEEPS TO ITSELF
MY THOUGHTS OF IMMORTALITY.

TAOS PUEBLO SONG, INTERPRETED BY NANCY WOOD

It felt like a coffin. I was lying on my back in what appeared to be a shallow grave. It was two feet deep and lined with old rocks. As I lay there, watching the blue-white midday sky, a dark form silhouetted itself high in the stratosphere, flying in from the east, the direction my head pointed. Another one came in from the same direction. They began to circle each other lazily, and tightened the spiral until they were almost touching. Suddenly, one of the forms flipped over. The move was startling in its contrast to their smooth flight. Talons locked, they plummeted in freefall, flipping over like a critically injured kite. They separated, and began again to capture the updrafts in slow flight.

I was in the prairie badlands of North Dakota. When I had first spotted the old eagle-catching pit, far below a high bluff, I scrambled down to it immediately. I lay down inside from curiosity. I wanted to know what those young Mandan boys had felt, maybe 500 years ago, during their rite of passage into the world of the adult. In order to allow their own spirits to travel to Father Sky, they had to lure an eagle messenger down to them. The pit was covered with vegetation and a tethered live rabbit sat above the boy, as bait. When an eagle struck, there could be no mistakes. If the bird was not grabbed exactly right, above the powerful talons, there could easily be crippling injury. I tried to feel the euphoria and adrenaline they must have felt, knowing the danger and opportunity that came with the Eagle. If they were successful, they would pull two tail feathers, a gift from the spirit world, and let the Eagle return to the sky, their gift to the Wind and the Sun.

They usually lay in the pit for four days, knowing that the Eagle would not come with their new name until their own sacrifice was complete. I was given the gift of the Eagle mating dance only minutes after I lay down. It was up to me to make sense of that pleasant surprise. I'm still working on it.

Eagles were the emissaries from the sky. Eagle feathers were sacred pieces of spirit—never worn as casual adornment, but as reflections of a person's vision and accomplishments. They were expressions of bravery, good judgment, humility and special perspective. Feathers were, and are, constant prayers floating on the wind, back and forth from our world to another, invisible to us. Eagle feathers are the dreams of the seer, the freedom of choices, the link between the material and the ether. The flight of the Eagle is the release of our earthbound nature, and the joyous passage to the next world. When we transcend any of our human limitations, we fly with the Eagle.

The Iroquois thought of Eagle as a benevolent Cloud Spirit, who carries dew between his shoulders and sprinkles it on the people when they have need. All across the Great Plains, Native Americans think of the Eagle as the visionary, the one who sees the world far from itself with clarity and understanding. The eastern morning sky is golden, the color of the Sun's fire on the Eagle's back. Morning is the time of birth of a day, and illumination of the world. On the Medicine Wheel, Eagle is the seer, the one who calmly, patiently and clearly can assess a situation and act well in the face of distraction. The Eagle's eyes miss nothing.

Warriors called for help in their work with a whistle made of the wing-bone of an Eagle. Shamans would extract bad spirit through a sucking tube made of Eagle bone, confident that those negative forces could not withstand the clear vision of the Eagle. Eagle talons grip stronger than any other creature's hand, and were worn as an amulet to represent strength of character.

It is sad irony that environmentally aware white Americans want to protect the eagle so badly they resent traditional uses by a people who lived harmoniously with Eagle for thousands of years. How did Eagle become so rare and endangered? A white American might point to the obvious, the unrestricted killing, the use of poisons for insect control. But Native people know better. Eagle represents vision and a connection with the spirit world. Eagle is a reminder that connections are far more important than differences, and a people that forgets this will have little need for messengers between worlds. The Eagle is almost gone because it does not feel needed or wanted. It is waiting for our enlightenment.

Once long ago, according to Ojibwe tradition, medicine societies began to use their power for selfish reasons. They made people fear them, distorted and took the lives of others for personal gain. The Creator was angry at the twisted sickness on Earth, and decided to destroy everything after four days had passed. Just before dawn on the fourth day, Eagle flew from the space between dark and light, up toward the Creator. He screamed his song four times to get Creator's attention. Creator agreed to hold the dawn until Eagle had held council with him.

Eagle admitted to Creator that the world was full of evil, but he also said he had seen a few humans who had remained true to the teachings of kindness and harmony. Here and there the sacred tobacco smoke still rose from a lodge. Eagle saw humility in the ways of a few people, and pleaded with the Creator to call off the coming destruction in their name. He offered a deal. If Eagle could fly over the Earth and report every day to Creator that there were still some who followed the good road, Creator would not destroy the world. If there was someone doing a good deed, sounding the Drum, observing the Sacred Circle through the Pipe, or thinking of the unborn, Eagle would report to Creator that there was still hope in the world. Creator agreed, saying that the deeds of the born should not overrule the promise of the unborn. Eagle still flies to the Sun every day. I wonder if things look better now than they did before. . .

A Zuni Pueblo boy found an Eagle nestling which had fallen from its cliff home. He took the bird home and spent most of his time hunting for this bird and caring for it. His parents and relatives became very upset that the boy spent little time helping in the fields, and they decided to kill the Eagle. Eagle knew what was about to happen (he could see all the way out to the fields) and told the boy he was sad that things had worked out like this. He told the boy he must leave, for everyone's good. The boy was distraught, and begged the Eagle to take him along. After much discussion, Eagle finally agreed, but the boy had to agree to pack much food and tie bells to the feet of Eagle. They left at dawn.

Eagle Boy climbed on the back of Eagle and they rose high into the sky. The bells were jingling and they sang a flight song. The relatives down below cried and begged the boy to come home, but he didn't hear them. Eagle and Eagle Boy flew through a hole in the clouds and landed on the Sacred Mountain of the Eagle People. These People adopted the Boy and made him a flying coat of feathers. He soon learned to fly as they did.

The Eagle People told Eagle Boy that he should never fly to the Land of Bones in the south, but his curiosity was too great for his judgment. He flew over the Land of Bones at night and saw beautiful people dancing around beautiful fires in a beautiful city. He flew down to join them and danced until he was exhausted. He fell asleep. When he woke in the morning, all he saw were dusty crumbling buildings and piles of bones. He looked for his coat of feathers, to fly away, but it was gone. Suddenly, the bones stood up and were skeletons. They chased him into the den of a badger, who told the boy of a way he could climb back to the Eagle People. It took a long time, but he finally arrived at the Sacred Mountain again. The Eagle People told him he was no longer welcome there, and turned away from him. His Eagle friend took pity on him and gave him a tattered feather coat, so he could fly home to the Pueblos. He just made it—the coat disintegrated as soon as he landed. He never went back, but remembers the place above the clouds every time he sees the Eagles high overhead.

The Vision Quest of young boys and girls, and the fasting and praying of anyone else, is symbolized by the spiritual flight to the home of the Eagle. It is a metaphor for transcending the limitations of the material world. What we learn there is ours alone, and we should live consistently within our calling. Becoming adult, in both the literal and figurative senses, has to do with learning that we are capable, significant and gifted in a unique way. Our peace with ourselves comes through that self-knowledge and the skills we acquire as we age. The "higher self" we call upon for good judgment, social skills and understanding of our role in systems comes from our spiritual visits to "Eagle Land," the risky places where we must go to grow. As parents, we must also remember that children are never born in our image. They have their own role to fulfill in this world, and we must let them go—from our expectations of *ourselves*.

Long ago, when all the Peoples spoke the same language, the first Abenaki man formed himself from the dust which Creator had not used in the rest of creation. This naked Dust Man lived with his Grandmother Woodchuck. One day he was hungry, and wanted to shoot some ducks out on the lake. He paddled out in his canoe, but the wind blew him back to the shore. He tried again, and the wind blew him back. He tried a third and fourth time, with the same result. He went back to his Grandmother's lodge and asked her where the wind comes from. She did not want to answer him because she knew that his curiosity usually led to trouble. But she also knew he would not stop asking, so she told him about the Wind Eagle who flapped his wings from the top of the tallest mountain. He asked how to find this Eagle. She sighed and told him to walk into the wind, and he would find the Wind Eagle.

Dust Man walked into the wind and as he came closer to the mountains, the wind blew stronger and stronger. As he climbed, the wind blew off his moccasins, then his shirt, his breechcloth, and finally his hair. He shouted at Wind Eagle, "Grandfather!" The Wind Eagle stopped flapping his wings. Dust Man praised Wind Eagle and asked him if he might not be even better at making wind from a peak to the west. Wind Eagle asked how he could possibly get over there and Dust Man offered to carry him. Wind Eagle thought it was worth a try. Dust Man made a rope of twisted basswood bark, and tied Wind Eagle tight in order to carry him. They were halfway down the mountain and Dust Man dropped Wind Eagle into a crevice. "Now I can hunt ducks," he said.

As Dust Man traveled home, he became very hot in the still air. The lake began to rot and the fish and ducks died. Dust Man asked his Grandmother what was wrong. She asked him what he had done. He finally admitted what he had done to the Wind Eagle. She told him that without the wind spirits, the Earth would be out of balance, and it would die. She encouraged him to make things right with the Eagle. He waited until his hair grew back and the Eagle would not recognize him, then he went to the crevice and the Eagle was there, stuck upside down in the crack. "Uncle!" he said. "What happened?"

Eagle told him of the ugly naked man who had tricked him and thrown him into the crevice. Dust Man climbed down and pulled him out. Dust Man asked him if it might not be better if the wind blew on some days, and not on others. The Eagle looked at him hard and said, "Perhaps it would. . .*Grandson.*"

The spiritual side of all Peoples, that mysterious wind moving through all things, is a part of the world that renews and refreshes the harmony of life. A world without spirit is a stagnant and rotting world. Systems die, species become endangered, and people turn on each other to victimize and blame. For short-term personal gain, we decide that our spiritual side is in the way of our well-being, and we throw it into the crevice. If we are to be here, if we are to leave a world fit for our children's children, we will have to pull it back out some day.

The spirit world is a place where Eagle flies every day, and his connection to departed spirits was assumed. In a Yakima story, Coyote and Eagle were both mourning the death of relatives. Coyote decided to comfort Eagle by pointing out that even the plants which die in the fall are making room for new flowers and leaves. The dead also feed the new, he said. But Eagle was not consolable. He wanted his dead relatives back right now. He talked Coyote into going with him back to the land of the dead. They traveled a long time, and finally came to a huge lake, with houses on the other side. Coyote called for a boat, but no one answered. They waited until dark, and Coyote began to sing a special song. Four people made of fog came out of a house and began to paddle their canoe over to Coyote and Eagle. They kept time with Coyote's song as they paddled.

They arrived at the village on the other side and the Fog People warned Coyote and Eagle not to look to the side in this sacred place, only straight ahead. Coyote asked if they could at least go into a lodge and have something to eat. The Fog People took them inside and fed them. The next night, Coyote stood next to the moon as the Spirit People woke up and began to dance. Coyote swallowed the moon, and in the confusion, Eagle gathered up all the Fog People and put them into a basket coyote carried. They closed the lid tightly.

As Coyote carried the Spirit People closer to the land of the living, they began to come to life and talk inside the basket. The basket became much heavier, because live people weigh more than spirits. Coyote had to stop and rest more often as the basket became heavier and heavier. He finally said to Eagle, "We should let them out to walk by themselves. They will never find their way back now."

It took some convincing, but Eagle finally agreed. They opened the lid and the Spirit People immediately flew like wind back to their village across the lake. Eagle was disappointed, and asked Coyote to go back and try again. Coyote refused, saying that the weight of the dead would be too much for the living, and that people should stay in the other world when they die.

Eagle saw the logic in Coyote's argument, but he still flies to the Spirit World each day, to bring messages back and forth. If we miss someone, we can trust Eagle to bring them that comforting message. And sometimes the Fog People just want us to know that it's OK over there.

With the slicing vision of Eagle, we can avoid being blinded by fear of the unknown. Eagle moves like Wind, through all worlds and all things, circling the Sun, reporting on our condition. With the help of all the Peoples, feathered, finned, legged and green, some of us will remember to have pipe smoke coming from our lodges. For now, it's still OK over here, too. For now.

This chapter is dedicated to the memory of helicopter pilot David Walton, who, ironically, I never met but continues to gently touch me through his friends. He circles slowly over us almost every day.

109

Chapter Ten

Moving Grace and Saying Grace

I HAD NEED.
I HAVE DISPOSSESSED YOU OF BEAUTY, GRACE, AND LIFE.
I HAVE TAKEN YOUR SPIRIT FROM ITS WORLDLY FRAME.
NO MORE WILL YOU RUN IN FREEDOM
BECAUSE OF MY NEED.

I HAD NEED.
YOU HAVE IN LIFE SERVED YOUR KIND IN GOODNESS.
BY YOUR LIFE, I WILL SERVE MY BROTHERS AND SISTERS.
WITHOUT YOU I HUNGER AND GROW WEAK.
WITHOUT YOU I AM HELPLESS, NOTHING.

I HAD NEED.
GIVE ME YOUR FLESH FOR STRENGTH.
GIVE ME YOUR COVERING FOR PROTECTION.
GIVE ME YOUR BONES FOR MY LABORS.
AND I SHALL NOT WANT.

OJIBWE PRAYER TO A SLAIN DEER

In western society we have a relatively new movement, which assumes that life is sacred. Traditional peoples would agree, in part. But, thinking only as far back as breakfast, they would also remind us that death is sacred too, as is soil formation from dead bodies, killing, eating, defecating and all of the other processes of the universe. No matter what our philosophical point of departure, we must force ourselves to look through a wide-angle lens.

The assumption of Native peoples, a logical one from a perspective of equality, was that all beings deserved life. This led to a paradox, especially concerning the whitetail deer. In order for humans to live, some deer had to die.

If there is a recurring theme in Native American stories about deer, it is one of reconciliation of this paradox. If animals were ever taken for granted, they would be justifiably insulted, and refuse to give themselves to humans thereafter. The subtle message here is that deer make choices too. Instead of the human-centered view that "I can't hunt very well," there is a humble acknowledgment that the world has its own plan independent of our wishes. An unsuccessful hunter would more likely say "Deer don't want to die for me today."

A story from the Ojibwe is quite blunt about the human responsibility to be humble. The deer had vanished from the land of the Anishnabeg, and the humans roamed over the world in search of them. Owl, who often foretells things to come, found all the deer in a huge corral far to the north. They grazed and browsed as if nothing at all were wrong. The curious owl flew down to question the deer, but a flock of crows attacked the owl and drove it away. The owl escaped their beaks only because it was night, and it could see and hear better than the crows.

When the owl reported the location of the deer, the humans formed a large war party to rescue them. Owl guided them back to the gates of the enclosure, but they were surprised by an attack of the fierce crows. The battle lasted for days, but no side gained an advantage. The deer made no attempt to escape—they just watched.

Finally the chief of the humans asked for a truce, realizing that defeating the crows would cost as much in human suffering as in crow suffering. The crows laughed that humans would learn this lesson in such a difficult way.

Then the chief of the Anishnabeg asked the deer why they were so unconcerned about the rescue attempt, especially since the war party had suffered so much. The deer chief answered that they were in this place by choice—the crows had treated them much better than humans ever had.

Humans had wasted their flesh, spoiled their lands and desecrated their bones. The two-leggeds had dishonored the deer and therefore themselves. "Without you we can live very well, but without us you will die."

The Anishnabeg promised to stop offending the lives, deaths and spirits of the deer, and the deer followed the humans back to their lands. Today, they honor this as the oldest and most sacred treaty. It is unthinkable to forget where life originates—from the deer's gift of itself.

The Wintu people of northern California believed that the successful taking of a deer had a prerequisite level of skill, preparation and respect, but the crucial element was the choice made by the deer. If any part of the human responsibility—not wasting, humility, gratitude, courtesy—is forgotten, the deer will "forget" to show up next time.

The Cherokee believed that this level of respect had direct positive effects on individuals, and direct negative effects if the rites were not done in sincerity. A long time ago, humans and deer lived in peace. Humans hunted and killed deer only when they needed food and clothing. Then something happened which changed it all—humans invented bows and arrows. They could now kill at great distance, effortlessly. They began to kill unnecessarily, and the animals were afraid they would be eradicated. They had a meeting.

The bears made bows even stronger than the human bows, but their claws were too long to shoot the bows. When they removed their claws they could not climb trees. The bears decided against such a compromise.

The other animals met in their groups and attempted to find a way to fight the humans, but they had as little success as the bears. The last group to meet was the deer, whose leader was Awi Udsi, Little Deer. They realized there was no way to stop the humans from killing, but there might be a way to change the *way* they killed. Awi Udsi went to the humans in their sleep and told them that they must prepare for the hunt with rituals. They must ask permission to take a deer. They must ask for pardon from the deer's spirit after the kill. If they did not do *all* of these things, the meat from the deer would make them sick and crippled. Deer did have control of the quality of their meat.

A few hunters didn't believe that Awi Udsi was anything more than a dream and soon became crippled and sick. Those who understood the dream lesson—that everything is dependent on everything else—never took the presence of deer for granted, learned to say "grace" and never wanted for deer to eat.

Compared to bears, wolves, coyotes, spiders, eagles, hawks, bison and a number of other animals, deer aren't mentioned as often in Native lore. Considering their importance to human survival, this is somewhat surprising. It is entirely possible that including whitetail deer as characters in stories would be a risk—if the character were somehow offensive to the deer, the deer could withhold their flesh from human consumption. It would always be foolish to gamble with the whitetail's gracious gift of itself. Being discrete about deer is good politics.

There is, perhaps, another reason deer are scarce in Native lore. The deer hunters I know (at least the ones I respect) always feel some guilt when they take the life of a whitetail. Humans have a natural avoidance of uncomfortable topics, and it is difficult to explain the paradox a hunter feels between respect and admiration for a living deer, and the good taste of venison. If the wonderful attributes of the whitetail deer were celebrated too much, it could make the necessary duties of survival much more difficult.

There is also a chance that the deer may get revenge someday. Iktomi, the snare-weaver, is a sometimes-human-sometimes-spider character of the Lakota people. Iktomi is part young, naive bumbler and part crafty trickster, in the tradition of Coyote in the South and West. He always wants what he doesn't have, but can't seem to observe the conditions under which he is given new attributes (and there are *always* conditions). Toward the end of one story, after he has unsuccessfully tried to be a beautiful but flightless bird and an arrow who flies high but always comes down, Iktomi sees some playing fawns and begins to covet their beautiful brown and white spots.

"How did you get those wonderful spots?" he asked.

A fawn looked at Iktomi carefully, and answered that its mother marked its face with coals from a red hot fire. "She dug a hole in the ground for me and made a soft bed of grass and twigs in it. Then she covered me with sweet grass and dry cedars. From a fire she borrowed a large red ember and tucked it next to my face, to make the spots."

"Will you do the same for me?" Iktomi asked, still trying to be someone other than himself. The fawn agreed to do it, trying to keep a straight face.

"Make sure you pile extra grass and cedars on top of me, because I want better spots than you have," Iktomi demanded. The fawn was happy to accommodate. It put the hot coal among the dry grass and scampered away, leaving Iktomi to his self-imposed fate.

Aside from the lesson on being who we are, the message says that deer owe us nothing—we owe them.

Unusual animals of any species were treated conservatively. Often just the fact that an animal was out of the ordinary meant it must be present for a special reason, such as the delivery of a special message. It was best not to take chances, so these animals were seldom killed. Even though ordinary whitetail deer are infrequently mentioned in Native American lore, these special animals were treated differently. When I was a kid, I heard many stories about Native people and white buffalo. Albino bison were thought to have great powers, and the same is true of white deer.

The Umpqua people of southern Oregon owe a debt to the white deer. Once, a terrible disease spread through the Umpqua nation, killing hundreds of people. The medicine men and women of the Umpqua went to the top of the nearby Cascade mountains, somewhere near Crater Lake, to fast and pray that the diseasse would leave them. It didn't work, at least at first.

The most beautiful, graceful and competent young woman in the largest village, a chief's daughter named Teola, then became sick. No one ever recovered from this dread disease, and so the people were very sad, chanting the death songs or sitting quietly. A white deer came out of the dark forest and walked around the woman's lodge three times, each time looking in the door at Teola. The third time around, this deer walked inside and stretched its neck toward Teola. She reached her hand toward the white deer and touched its nose. Then the deer walked back into the forest. Teola sat up from her bed and was completely healed. Her movements became even more graceful, like the deer, as a constant reminder to the people of the white deer's gift.

Since that day, the Umpqua people never kill an albino deer for food. Some Umpqua are firm in their belief that the reason white society is so unsettled and environmentally harmful today is that they killed white deer indiscriminately. This showed the Great Mystery that they did not respect the world enough to look for messages from the rest of nature.

The Lakota people of the northern plains believe that white deer are the visible forms of strange people who live out in the wilds, or sometimes the form in which those who have died return to give us important messages. There are many stories of women pleading with a hunter to spare a white deer, usually because it is a departed relative. The general tempering message from women to men is to use those traditionally masculine powers wisely, and listen to the advice of women. Because of the female nurturing power, they will see things that are not obvious to men. These complementary perspectives are essential to a balanced view for all of us.

Perhaps one lesson the deer can bring to us even today is to listen, watch, be patient, consider irreversible decisions carefully—it is sometimes wise to *be* a deer.

CHAPTER ELEVEN

Loon
LOYALITY AND LEADERSHIP

LOONS
WHAT FORCE BROUGHT YOU TOGETHER
YOUR DESTINIES TO UNITE?
CHANCE? NATURE?

WHAT POWER DRAWS YOU IN FIDELITY
TO ENDURING HARMONY?
LOVE? NATURE?

WHAT ELEMENT CLEAVES ONE YOUR SOULS
IN THEIR SEPARATE BEINGS?
WILL? NATURE?

WHAT PURPOSE IMPELS YOUR SPIRITS ONE
ALONE TO RANGE THE REALMS?
FREEDOM? NATURE?

BASIL JOHNSTON, OJIBWE TEACHER

Loon music has been making the hair of humans stand up since humans had hair everywhere, and were yet to become bipeds. We have been walking on two legs for about three million years. Loons have been wailing their music for ten times longer. They are widely regarded as the eldest of the Elders, both by scientists, who put them on the first page of field guides, and by our human Elders on this continent. In thirty million years, Loons must have learned something. . .

The Ojibwe, who live across a wide expanse of North America, virtually all of it in loon country, have five original Midewewin (medicine society) Clans. The Loon Clan is the clan of bravery, honor and fidelity—perfect qualities for a leader. The Loon Clan is therefore the leadership clan of the Ojibwe.

It was not difficult for Native Americans who lived in lake country to notice loons. The males arrived just after ice-out, yodeling their loud, complex song for the benefit of everyone within miles. Native people watched the same male (they could tell because the yodel song is unique for each male) return to its nesting spot year after year. They knew that a loon's first allegiance is to its place, but if both loons in a pair returned, they "mated for life" by default. The metaphor of being first bonded to the land and then bonded to other relationships was not lost on them. A loon's fidelity was not just to another loon. Loyalties, to be healthy, should be spread around a bit, never blind, and never narrowed to just one part of creation.

The northern woods people watched loons dive for long periods to the mysterious world under the surface of a lake. They saw that loons were so much a part of the water that their legs could no longer help them walk. The legs were where a tail should be. Many believed that the Loon had done something to offend Creator, and had been condemned to live in the water forever. But most Native people saw the Loon's ability to swim and dive as a special gift.

The Ojibwe, in fact, feel that this ability of the Loon is the reason they, and we, are here.

Long ago, before there was anything as we know it now, Creator was alone. Creator began to feel lonely. He made the Sky on the first day, and the great Waters on the second day. He reached into his sack of raw materials and made things with fins and feathers to fill the Sky and the Water. This didn't seem like enough, so he made four-legged and many-legged things with paws and hooves and creeping legs. They swam in the water endlessly.

Toward the end of that second day, Creator was tired and perhaps a little crabby. He wanted to go home and rest. But he still had not emptied the

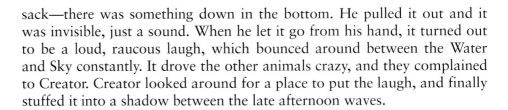

sack—there was something down in the bottom. He pulled it out and it was invisible, just a sound. When he let it go from his hand, it turned out to be a loud, raucous laugh, which bounced around between the Water and Sky constantly. It drove the other animals crazy, and they complained to Creator. Creator looked around for a place to put the laugh, and finally stuffed it into a shadow between the late afternoon waves.

On the third day of creation, Creator heard all the furred animals complaining that they were tired of swimming. Grandmother Turtle told Creator that she did not mind floating in the water, and that the animals could rest on her back if they wished. But Grandmother Turtle was small, and only one animal at a time could rest there. Creator realized that a lot of land would help the situation, and asked Goose to dive down and get some mud for him. Goose stretched her neck down but could not reach the bottom. Then muskrat tried. Then beaver tried. They could not reach the bottom either.

Finally, the Shadowy One with the loud laugh came by and Creator asked if he would be willing to try. Shadowy One was honored, but not very confident. He dove down and thought he had failed, but when he waved good-bye to Creator, some mud fell out of his huge foot. Creator used the mud to spread the back of Grandmother Turtle far across the Great Waters, making Turtle Island, where we live today. This took all day, exhausted Creator, and he went off to rest again. He knew he needed to rest because the fourth day of creation was to be a special one.

All of the fourth day, Creator worked on a special project, in secret. Meanwhile, over near Turtle Island, all the other animals were having a great time, laughing at the stupid Shadow with the silly laugh. They mocked the Shadowy One, and asked it in taunting tones, "Hah! What good are you? All you have as your gift is a useless laugh!"

Shadowy One was hurt and embarrassed. He was so embarrassed, his eyes turned red. As the animals kept mocking him he realized that the mocking was not so loud if he just put his head under the water. He could still hear it, but only faintly. Then he realized that maybe he could shut out the taunting completely if he dove deep. It worked. The animals kept taunting when he emerged, so all day he kept diving deeper and longer. He became quite good at it.

Toward the end of the fourth day, Creator presented his special project to the other creatures. This special project had a smooth body, long black hair on its head, and it walked on two legs. It was Anishnabe, the first human animal. The most special thing about this animal was its brain. As time went on, the other animals watched Anishnabe as he easily learned how to run, like a deer, or hunt, like a wolf, or swim, like an otter, or stalk, like a cougar. Then he started to make tools—bows and arrows, knives, baskets and scrapers—this was the most amazing thing they had ever seen! They praised Anishnabe constantly, telling him they wanted him to be the chief of all the animals, and how he was the most wonderful animal of all.

Anishnabe's ego began to grow, and he decided that, yes, he was the most wonderful animal of all. In fact, there wasn't *anything* he couldn't do. He announced to the animals that next, he was going to fly. The birds took one look at his bare body and were skeptical. The animals worried as he climbed to the top of a tall cliff overlooking a lake and got ready to fly. "Watch this," he said proudly, with his nose in the air. He jumped.

Of course he went straight down, like a rock, into the lake. He kept sinking deeper and deeper because he was fuming about his first failure. Down at the bottom of the lake, in the mud, lived the old trees which had sunk there in the first days of creation. They had long, algae-covered branches and finger-like twigs. They did not like the vibrations of anger and arrogance coming from this sinking creature. They decided to teach this thing a lesson, and grabbed Anishnabe by his long, beautiful hair. Then he was really angry, and he thrashed around, telling the trees that they could not do this to the most wonderful animal of all. He only tangled himself worse.

On the surface, the other animals were wringing their paws and hooves and talons, worried that their chief would never return. Goose, Muskrat and Beaver tried to reach him, but couldn't. Then the Shadowy One swam close, and quietly volunteered to try. "Hah! You? You are the useless one with the stupid laugh!"

"But, I can try." He dived down, down, down, to where Anishnabe was still thrashing, but getting weaker. Shadowy One started to cut the tangled hair but Anishnabe was very vain, and didn't want anyone to change his beautiful hair. So, very patiently, Shadowy One untangled every strand.

A little later, Anishnabe and Shadowy One popped to the surface. The animals cheered. Anishnabe walked ashore, his nose in the air, muttering to himself that he was the most wonderful animal of all, and he deserved to be saved. He did not even turn around to thank the Shadowy One.

Creator had been watching. He wanted to give this little shadow a gift for his bravery, but when he reached down in the sack, there were only leftovers from that fourth day of creation. There were only some slivers of white light—light which Creator had wanted to put in the heart of Anishnabe. But Creator decided that Shadowy One deserved them more, so he sprinkled some on the back of the Shadow, and then wove some pieces together and placed a necklace on the Shadowy One. As he did this, he said to the Shadow, "Shadowy One, you are truly 'mahng'" (which means "brave" in the Ojibwe language). Shadowy One thought that Creator was giving him a new name. "I'm Mahng! I'm Mahng! I'm Mahng!" he kept singing. Creator just smiled, and said he could keep the name.

Today, Loon has red eyes, white slivers on his back and a beautiful necklace. The Ojibwe language is usually very specific, but there is at least one word which has two separate meanings—the word Mahng. It means brave and courageous, but it also means Loon. When an Ojibwe says you are "loon-hearted," it is the highest compliment you can be given.

Anishnabe, and his descendants, haven't changed much. The two-legged arrogant animal still takes his origins, his dependency on the rest of creation, for granted. He still believes that the world was created just for him, and that he is far superior to the other animals. It remains to be seen how many times he can jump off a cliff before the other creatures give up on him. . .

The Copper and Dogrib Natives of the Northwest Territories, the Koyukon of Alaska, and the Tsimshian of British Columbia, have a story about a blind boy who is given his sight back by Loon. He takes the boy to the water underworld four times, each time the boy's sight becomes clearer. As a gift for this "vision quest," the boy makes Loon a necklace of white shells.

The haunting songs of the Loon have many meanings to loons, but people have their own interpretations. Many tribes believed that loon calls were the cries of slain warriors, or a hero who drowns while trying to rescue a lover. The Micmac believe that the call of the Loon is a message from Creator, to help them in their loneliness for their Maker. The Koyukon say that their songs are half Loon songs and half human songs.

The eerieness of the Loon's song was a handy tool for Skokomish parents. They told their children that once there was a sacred lake where the spirits lived. A mother warned her son never to go into that lake, or anywhere around it. The boy was curious and went swimming in the lake despite his mother's warnings. It was a beautiful day, and the boy caught a fat trout with only his hands. He ate the trout, and immediately turned into a Loon. He went crying back to his mother, who didn't recognize him any more and drove him away with a big stick. He still calls to his mother from the lake today.

This approach to parenting sounds a little manipulative and dishonest, but it was part of a broader message to the whole culture. Elders had the benefit of experience, and deserved respect. The older a person was, the more deference they deserved. Contrast that to our culture today. We worship eternal youth. We waste wisdom.

All across Inuit (Eskimo) country, there are variants on a story about how the birds were painted. Loon and Raven decided to do the painting of the other birds and then paint each other. All goes well with the other birds, and Raven paints Loon a beautiful black and white pattern. When Loon paints Raven, he can not convince Raven to sit still, and the paint job is not as good. Loon gets angry at Raven for squirming and throws ashes on him, turning him all black. Raven slices off Loon's tongue and throws stones at Loon's legs, breaking them. Then he throws Loon into the water. With no tongue, Loon can not speak, and with broken legs, he can not get out of the water. Thus began Loon's career as a shaman from the deep.

The early human, according to the Lakota, was represented by Little Boy Man, the first two-legged made by Creator. Early in his life, Little Boy Man was captured by a giant water monster. At first, Creator did not know who had taken Little Boy Man, but then he heard the monster

126

bragging to his mate about making the human's skin into a door flap. Creator made himself into a swallow so he could come to Earth, and he sought out the help of the great shaman of the deep, the Loon. Even Creator addressed Loon very respectfully. Loon was happy to teach the Swallow some powerful songs which would get him down into the underwater world. With the help of Snake and Turtle, Swallow found the skin and the bones of Little Boy Man. With another song taught to him by Loon, Swallow wrapped the skin around the bones and reformed Little Boy Man over four days.

Loon medicine continues to be powerful to this day. To many people, there is no sound more wild than the song of a Loon. They are the best of parents, sharing equally in the raising of their young and defending them with a courage that only a Mahng could muster. They are magic, but until a human has heard one on a still evening in Loon country, they will never understand how that song is the raw material for their own dreams and visions. Loon medicine, from our eldest shaman, still heals and soothes a torn heart.

CHAPTER TWELVE

TRICKSTER'S LITTLE SIBLING

FOX, LURKING IN THE NIGHT,
I SEE YOUR EYES.
GO TELL THE GROWING MOON
THAT MY MIND IS DARK.

POMO SONG

STOP. I SEE SOMETHING.
FAR AWAY THERE IS A FLASH OF FIRE.
YOU DID NOT SEE ME. . .
A FOX BOUNCES BRIGHTLY THROUGH THE BRUSH.

KOYUKON RIDDLE

S ometimes stories are just stories.

With very few exceptions, Fox is not thought of as a powerful spirit being by Native Americans (keeping in mind that *all* beings have some spiritual gift to offer). Foxes are small, secretive, nocturnal, and usually shy critters. They visit humans to steal scraps, but mostly they are seen at a distance, minding their own business. That "business" is usually leaping high in the air to pounce on voles in the grass, or sneaking wide-eyed toward a feeding rabbit. When they trot, it seems as if they have no weight at all. They are a "light" animal with a light demeanor. They beg not to be taken too seriously.

Maybe that is why Fox is often in stories, but seldom as the central character. Perhaps Native people saw in Fox an indifferent air, and Fox's lightness of being translated to humility—Fox didn't feel a need to be the central focus.

I don't believe it for a second. When I wake up on a winter morning, the straight lines of Fox tracks are everywhere in the snow. The Koyukon people have a respectful and indirect "name" for most animals which they use when handling their bodies. Fox is "Many Tracks," suggesting that she is in the vicinity, and involved, more than we think. We have also heard of the "sly" Fox, being "out-foxed," and speak of people who are "dumb like a fox." With the attention focused somewhere else, Fox is free to play her role as Coyote's apprentice. Fox is Coyote's little brother, or sometimes sister, and despite the fact that her powers are smaller, and not quite as dangerous, she still has the inclination to follow her brother's lead. The Koyukon are appropriately wary of Fox. When they kill her, they put a bone in her mouth and burn her carcass away from their village. That way, she won't take offense at being killed, and will be content on the other side. Take no chances. Fox could someday graduate from her apprenticeship.

Most of the Northern Native people believe that foxes barking at night foretell a death in their family. But Fox's magic is not that powerful. If the person hearing the Fox yells back, "Go die yourself!" the spell is broken. Fox's magic is still developing. . .

An Inuit tale hints at the tendency toward trickery in Fox. Bear was carrying a ground squirrel home for dinner when he met Fox on the trail. As Fox walked by, she whispered just loud enough for Bear to hear, "I'm more clever than you." Bear spun around and asked Fox to repeat what she had said. Fox pretended to be coy about it, but eventually repeated what she had whispered.

Bear challenged Fox to trick him on a bet. Fox told Bear she had nothing to bet except her clothes. Bear said that would do, and bet his ground squirrel. Fox then looked past Bear and asked if they could have the contest later, because something big was coming. Bear looked behind himself. Nothing was there. The contest was over almost before it started.

Another Inuit story told in Siberia and North America tells of the time that Fox trades a sack of "salt" for a caribou. The sack contains snow, which doesn't melt until Fox is long gone with the caribou.

Fox's tricks are usually more harmless than Coyote's. Often, Fox just gets herself out of trouble brought on by curiosity. Another Inuit story has Fox trying to get a fish from two gulls perched on a log. She pretends to yell to them, but uses a quiet voice. They flap their wings and move closer to the shore in order to hear Fox. Fox doesn't have quite enough patience and leaps too soon, landing in the water near the log. The gulls fly away with the fish.

Now Fox has a new problem. She climbs onto the log, paddles with her paws and steers with her tail. The current is too strong, and pulls her out to sea. She meets a Seal, and says that she thought seals were almost gone from the sea. The Seal says that there are many creatures out here, including the Walruses and Whales. Fox says she doesn't believe the Seal, but the sea animals could prove how many there were by lining up, in a row, so Fox could count them. They stretched in a line all the way to the shore, and Fox bounced on each one as she counted "one, two, three, four. . ." all the way to the shore. "You were right!" she yelled at Seal. "There are a great many of you, but none are very smart!"

The Kutchin and Yellowknife people of Northern Canada probably watched foxes pouncing out on the tundra, and have a story to account for how often the foxes miss their prey. Mouse and Fox were once friends, and they often played together.

One day Fox decided to have a contest she knew she could win. "Let's see who can jump the highest," she said. Fox won easily, and the result humiliated Mouse. Mouse then suggested hide-and-seek, and told Fox she could hide first. Fox hid, but her red bushy tail with the white tip was easy to spot. Mouse found her right away. Fox was disappointed, but waited for Mouse to hide. Fox looked everywhere, but Mouse was so small that he was invisible. Finally, Fox felt the same humiliation as Mouse had, of losing in a game where the odds were stacked against her. "I'm over here!" said Mouse, from under the grass. Fox jumped high in the air and pounced on the spot. "No, I'm over here!" he said from another place. Fox kept pouncing on Mouse's voice, and does so to this day.

Fox is not a good loser, as is shown in another Eskimo story. Fox saw some Ducks swimming toward her, and decided to hitch a ride to the point on the far side of the bay. Fox called to them, and went on and on about being very important, the mistress of this area, and what a privilege it would be for Ducks to float Fox across the water to the far point. The Ducks agreed, and made a raft for Fox. About halfway across, the Ducks flew in every direction, and Fox had to swim. Today, foxes rarely come down to the sea.

Native stories often "explain" why something is the way it is. Western minds, with a logical scientific explanation for the same phenomenon, often look at the Native story as childlike and stupid. When presented with the scientific explanation, traditional Native people will often nod their head, and politely say "that is a good story too." They have absolutely no desire to find a "reason" for what they observe—it just always happens that way, and they know it. Whatever story we prefer doesn't change the happening, so why not have an enjoyable "reason" for what we observe? Stories are just stories, after all.

Western Society takes itself very seriously, searching for "truth" in the scientific sense. These "truths" are the building blocks of flawless prediction and control of our environment, a philosophy with mixed results, at best. Native people look at their "truth" and its effects on this planet, and then look at Western "truth" and compare the resulting effects on our environment. When they say "That is a good story, too," they are being more than polite. . .

One such "explanation" story from the Inuit deals with the rivalry between Arctic foxes (Round-Ears) and red foxes. They eat many of the same foods and compete for the same space in the Far North. Fox was perturbed with the many times Round-Ears had won the race to food. She saw Round-Ears one day, and immediately went over to a huge cliff with an overhang, pushed her back up against the cliff, and yelled at Round-Ears for help. "What's the matter?" he asked. Fox explained that the cliff was ready to fall and kill them both, but she knew where to find some rocks to wedge into the cliff and fix it. If Round-Ears would just hold the cliff up while she fetched the rocks, they could both be safe. He agreed. She left, chuckling under her breath, and never came back. In the spring, Round-Ears often has a bare patch on his shoulder, where the fur has rubbed off from pushing so hard on the cliff. In the western world, we call the bare patch "the molt," the changing of long winter hairs for short summer hairs. That's a good story, too.

Sometimes, Fox is over her head in the trickery business. In a Tanana story, Fox finds a Bird in a tree nest. She has four nestlings, and Fox demands one of them to eat, threatening to chop down the tree with a "sword" in her tail "sheath." She throws one down, and Fox goes away to eat it. Raven flies by, and asks the Bird where the fourth nestling is. She relates the whole story. Raven points out that the Fox's tail is just a tail, and she should refuse him next time.

Fox comes back with the same ruse, but this time the Bird refuses him. Fox flails at the tree with her tail, but doesn't even make the tree shiver. Fox demands to know who told the Bird about her tail. She doesn't answer, but Fox thinks it must be Raven who exposed her trickery. She finds Raven's tent, digs a hole nearby on the top of a tall cliff, gets in the hole, and rolls out her red tongue. Raven takes the bait, and Fox grabs him. "I'll teach you a lesson now!" she says. Raven apologizes and begs for mercy. "Do anything to me you want, but please don't push me off that cliff! Please!"

Fox thinks to herself, "That's exactly what I'll do. . ." She steps back and runs at Raven, who Flaps into the air at the last minute. Fox can't stop, and tumbles off the cliff. No one should try to out-raven Raven. . .

The Crow People tell a story of how Fox once tried to out-coyote Coyote, too. Coyote tricked two Buffalo into racing him into the Sunset. He slowed down and let them pass. They were blinded by the sun and ran over a cliff, killing themselves. Coyote was about to skin and butcher them when Fox showed up. Coyote wanted some Buffalo soup, and had left his spoon, a Cougar paw, at the starting point of the race. Coyote demanded that Fox go get the spoon, and if she did, she could have some soup. Fox showed Coyote the bottoms of her moccasins, which were nearly worn out. Coyote grumbled and said that he would get the spoon if Fox would do the butchering. When Coyote came back, of course, the meat was gone.

Coyote tracked Fox to where she was sleeping in the grass. He tied her tail to a stake, and set the grass on fire. She jumped up and ran away, feeling something snap behind her. Coyote began to laugh at her because she looked so silly without a tail. She was embarrassed, and asked Coyote what she could do to get her tail back. He laughed because her trick was almost as good as a Coyote trick. He told her that she could have the tail back if she always ate after Coyote, if he was around. So she would not forget, he put some white grass smoke on the end of her tail. It is still there today, reminding Fox that she is still the apprentice.

Fox is an expert at finding the buried food caches of other animals, and when they are not around, she digs up the food and eats it. Interestingly, when a fox buries food itself, it rarely remembers to go back and eat it. Other foxes usually find it first.

But it is important to remember that Fox and Coyote are siblings, and when they take on a task together, they are a formidable pair. A Salish story tells about a Whale who came up the Columbia River and stole the wife of Fox (in this story he is male). Fox was so distraught, he starved himself and became very thin. Coyote was concerned about his little sibling and tried to help by planning to get Fox's wife back. Coyote thought that water-food would not be enough to keep a land woman healthy, and they should wait until someone came to steal food. Sure enough, two young Water-Women came in a short canoe to steal dried meat. Fox and Coyote surprised them, learned where Fox's wife was kept, and killed the two Water-Women.

They dressed in the clothes of the two women, grabbed some packs of food and went in the strange canoe to the bottom of the rapids. The huge and terrible Whale lived there. He was the chief of the Water People. Fox and Coyote fed the Whale and his wife, and when they were asleep, Fox let out a loud war cry and cut off the head of the giant Whale. He slashed so hard that the Whale's body began to spin in the water. It dug a hole in the river and formed Big Falls. Coyote grabbed the woman and Fox carried the head of the Whale. Their weight was too much for the strange canoe, so Coyote stuffed everyone into his Medicine Pipe and they escaped. The body of the Whale washed to the sea and was a warning for all whales that they were no longer welcome up the river in Coyote's land. Strong Medicine and cunning are always a match for brute force. Especially when we cooperate.

The Miwok say that Fox and Coyote have been a team since the beginning. In the distant time, Fox was the only one around. She was lonely, and began to sing a song about wanting to meet someone. Coyote showed up. Fox was pleased with Coyote and they decided to travel together. This was fine for a while, but then Fox was restless and asked Coyote if he wanted to make the world. Coyote asked how they would do that, and Fox said, "We will sing the world."

They began to sing and dance in a circle, and after a while Fox said, "Clump of sod, clump of sod, go down there." A small piece of sod fell down into a fog and settled.

Coyote thought that the clump was too small to dance on, so they kept dancing in a circle with their eyes closed, singing the World. As they sang, they danced in a bigger and bigger circle, spreading the sod just in front of where they stepped. They stretched the World, and sang the plants and animals to fill it. It was a good place. It still is.

EPILOGUE

SOMETIMES I GO ABOUT PITYING MYSELF,
BUT ALL THE WHILE
I AM BEING CARRIED BY GREAT WINDS
ACROSS THE SKY. . .

OJIBWE SONG

After Creator was done with most of creation, he made two very special things. He called them Love and Honor, because they were made of most of the good feelings Creator had for the World. But he had one worry. It was the two-leggeds. He knew they could take Love and Honor and twist them for selfish reasons. He knew they could make things seem like Love and Honor when they really weren't. He asked the animals for help.

At dawn, Eagle came soaring from the East. He offered to fly the special creations far up into the sky—even to the Moon. "That will be a good hiding place," he told Creator.

The Creator thought about Eagle's offer for a while, but then shook his head.

"They will find them there," he said. "One day, another Eagle will land on the Moon. It will have two-leggeds inside, and they will find the Special Gifts."

About noon, Mouse scurried to Creator from his home in the South. He offered to take the Gifts and bury them under the vast expanse of grass on the prairie. "That will confuse them. The prairie is too big."

Creator thought this idea might work, but then he shook his head.

"No," he said. "These two-leggeds will some-day turn over the whole prairie with their iron plows. They will leave no room for the First People or the Buffalo. They will find the Gifts."

At sunset, Bear lurched to where Creator sat, huffing his way from his home in the West. He offered to take the Gifts to the high mountains and dig a deep cave. "If I put them there, the rocks will be too hard for the two-leggeds to dig, and they will give up."

Creator thought, and then shook his head again.

"Those two-leggeds are resourceful," he said. "One day they will take giant machines and dig the rock away. They will be looking for shiny things—things that will make them crazy. They will find the Gifts because they will dig holes in the Earth as big as the mountains."

When it was dark, the night cooled the air, and Wolf loped to where Creator sat. He came from his home in the far North. Wolf offered to take the Gifts to the farthest North spot. He could bury the Gifts in the huge sheet of ice and it would never melt. "They will never want to go there," he said.

Creator pondered Wolf's offer for a while, and then, sadly, shook his head again.

"I think those two-leggeds will have a curiosity which will make them do things just because they can," he said to Wolf. "They will not ask themselves if they *should*, because they will be so enamored with their skills. I think they will make special boats that will go *under* the Great Ice, and they will find the gifts."

Creator sat until dawn, thinking. Just before the sun rose again, Mole pushed his strange fingered nose from the ground, between Creator's feet. Mole was startled at first, but then greeted Creator, and asked him what was troubling him. Creator explained the problem.

Mole was quiet for a while, but then spoke to Creator. "I know I am just a small Mole, and you are the Creator. I know you have asked the wisest animals in the Great Medicine Wheel to help you and they could not. I only know about the insides of the Earth, the insides of things, but I have an idea. Why don't you take the Gifts of Love and Honor and bury them deep inside the *hearts* of these two-leggeds. They will *never* find them there. . ."

Creator did. And you know, to this day, the only two-leggeds who have found them are the ones who know where to look.

REFERENCES

deAngulo, Jaime. *Indian Tales*. New York: Hill & Wang Pub. & Ballantine Books, 1953.

Astrov, Margot, ed. *American Indian Prose and Poetry*. New York: Capricorn Books, 1946.

Benton-Benai, Edward. *The Mishomis Book*. St. Paul: Indian Country Press, 1979.

Brown, Joseph Epes. *The Spiritual Legacy of the American Indian*. New York: Crossroad Press, 1982.

———. *The Sacred Pipe*. Norman: University of Oklahoma Press, 1953.

Bruchac, Joseph. *Flying with the Eagle, Racing with the Great Bear*. Mahwah, N.J.: BridgeWater Books, 1993.

Caduto, Michael and Joseph Bruchac. *Keepers of the Animals*. Golden, Colo.: Fulcrum Publishing, 1991.

———. *Keepers of the Earth*. Golden, Colo.: Fulcrum Publishing, 1988.

———. *Keepers of the Night*. Golden, Colo.: Fulcrum Publishing, 1994.

Clark, Ella C. *Indian Legends of the Pacific Northwest*. Berkeley: University of California Press, 1953.

Courlander, Harold. *The Fourth Word of the Hopis*. Albuquerque: University of New Mexico Press, 1908.

Cronyn, George. *American Indian Poetry*. New York: Liveright Publishing, 1934.

Eastman, Charles E. *Indian Scout Craft and Lore*. New York: Little, Brown & Company, 1914.

———. *The Soul of the Indian*. Norman: University of Nebraska Press, 1911.

———. *Wigwam Evenings*. New York: Little Brown and Company, 1909.

Erdoes, Richard and Alfonso Ortiz. *American Indian Myths and Legends*. New York: Pantheon Books, 1984.

Furtman, Michael. *Sky Spirit: The American Bald Eagle*. Minocqua, Wis.: NorthWord Press, 1994.

Goodchild, Peter. *Raven Tales*. Chicago: Chicago Review Press, 1991.

Grim, John A. *The Shaman*. Norman: University of Oklahoma Press, 1963.

Hamilton, Virginia. *In the Beginning: Creation Stories*. New York: Harcourt Brace Jovanovich, 1988.

Harris, Lorle K. *Tlingit Tales*. Happy Camp, Calif.: Naturegraph Publishers, 1985.

Hausman, Gerald. *Turtle Island Alphabet*. New York: St. Martin's Press, 1992.

Hill, Ruth Beebe. *Hanta Yo*. New York: Doubleday & Company, 1979.

Holbrook, Florence. *The Book of Nature Myths*. New York: Houghton Mifflin & Co., 1902.

Hunter, Wilson. pers. com. Canyon du Chelley, Ariz., 1994.

Johnston, Basil. *Ojibway Ceremonies*. Lincoln: University of Nebraska Press, 1982.

———. *Ojibway Heritage*. Lincoln: University of Nebraska Press, 1976.

Klein, Tom. *Loon Magic*. Minocqua, Wis.: NorthWord Press, 1985.

Phil Lane et al. *The Sacred Tree*. Lethbridge, Alberta: Four Worlds Development Press, 1984.

Locke, Kevin. *The Flood and Other Lakota Stories*. Audio tape. New York: Harper Collins, 1993.

Lopez, Barry H. *Giving Birth to Thunder, Sleeping with His Daughter*. New York: Avon Books, 1977.

———. *Of Wolves and Men*. New York: Charles Scribner's Sons, 1978.

———. *Winter Count*. New York: Charles Scribner's Sons, 1981.

McClintock, Walter. *The Old North Trail*. Lincoln: University of Nebraska Press, 1910.

McGaa, Ed. *Mother Earth Spirituality*. San Francisco: Harper and Row, 1990.

McIntyre, Judith W. *The Common Loon: Spirit of Northern Lakes*. Minneapolis: University of Minnesota Press, 1988.

Morriseau, Norval. *Legends of My People: The Great Ojibway*. Toronto: McGraw-Hill, 1965.

Mourning Dove. *Coyote Stories*. Lincoln: Bison Books, Univ. of Nebraska, 1953.

Mullet, G. M. *Spider Woman Stories*. Tucson: University of Arizona Press, 1979.

Nelson, Richard K. *Make Prayers to the Raven*. Chicago: University of Chicago Press, 1983.

Nerburn, Kent and Louise Mengelkoch. *Native American Wisdom*. San Rafael, Calif.: New World Library, 1991.

Olson, Dennis L. *The Way of the Whitetail*. Minocqua, Wis.: NorthWord Press, 1994.

Olson, Sigurd F. *Runes of the North*. New York: Alfred A. Knopf, 1963.

Parker, Arthur C. *Seneca Myths and Folk Tales*. Lincoln: University of Nebraska Press, 1923.

Peyton, John L. *The Stone Canoe*. Blacksburg, Vir.: McDonald & Woodward Publishing, 1989.

Roberts, Elizabeth and Elias Amidon, eds. *Earth Prayers & Songs*. San Francisco: Harper Collins, 1991.

Rockwell, David. *Giving Voice to Bear*. Niwot, Colo.: Roberts Rinehart Publishers, 1991.

Shepard, Paul and Barry Sanders. *The Sacred Paw*. New York: Arkana Books, 1992.

Silko, Leslie Marmon. *Ceremony*. New York: Penguin Books, 1977.

Solasko, Fianna. *Kutkha the Raven*. Moscow: Malysh Publishers, 1976.

Storm, Hyemeyohsts. *Seven Arrows*. New York: Ballantine Books, 1972.

Strauss, Susan. *Tracks, Tracks, Tracks*. Audio tape. Bend, Ore.: Story Teller, 1989.

———. *Wolf Stories*. Hillsboro, Ore.: Beyond Words Publishing, 1993.

———. pers. com., 1992.

Suzuki, David and Peter Knudtson. *Wisdom of the Elders*. New York: Bantam Books, 1992.

Tedlock, Dennis, and Barbara Tedlock, eds. *Teachings from the American Earth*. New York: Liveright Press, 1975.

Vogel, Virgil J. *American Indian Medicine*. Norman: University of Oklahoma Press, 1970.

Waldman, Carl. *Atlas of the North American Indian*. New York: Facts on File Press, 1985.

Walker, Deward E. *Myths of Idaho Indians*. Moscow, Idaho: University of Idaho Press, 1980.

Wall, Steve, and Harvey Arden. *Wisdomkeepers*. Hillsboro, Ore.: Beyond Words Publishing, 1990.

Waters, Frank. *Book of the Hopi*. New York: Viking Press, 1963.

———. *Masked Gods*. Athens, Ohio: Swallow Press, 1950.

White Bear Woman. *BearWalker*. Audio tape. Minocqua, Wis.: NorthWord Press, 1994.

Williams, Terry Tempest. *Pieces of White Shell*. Albuquerque: University of New Mexico Press, 1983.

Wood, Douglas. pers. com., 1988.

Wood, Nancy. *Many Winters*. New York: Doubleday & Company, 1974.

———. *Spirit Walker*. New York: Doubleday & Company, 1993.

Zitkala-Sa. *Old Indian Legends*. Lincoln: University of Nebraska Press, 1901.